The Big FEARON Book of Teachers' Holiday Helpers

Halloween • Thanksgiving • Christmas
Valentine's Day • Springtime

Seasonal Activities for the Primary Grades

by Judy Beach and Kathleen Spencer

Fearon Teacher Aids
a division of
David S. Lake Publishers
Belmont, California

Entire contents copyright © 1987 by David S. Lake
Publishers, 19 Davis Drive, Belmont, California 94002.
Permission is hereby granted to reproduce designated
materials in this book for noncommercial classroom
and individual use.

ISBN 0-8224-6776-3

Printed in the United States of America

1. 9 8 7 6 5 4 3 2 1

Contents

Teacher Guide
Introduction 1
Bulletin Board Displays 2
Bulletin Board Patterns.............. 7
Calendar and Finger Play Guide 27

Activity Sheets

Halloween
Completing a calendar 31
Dramatizing a poem 32
Matching capital and
   lowercase letters 33
Identifying initial consonants 37
Identifying missing vowel letters......38
Recognizing similarities
   and differences 40
Identifying sequence of events 41
Using directional words 42
Writing creatively..................43
Recognizing shapes 44
Completing an art project 46
Identifying number sequence........47
Identifying number values 48
Practicing addition facts
   less than ten....................50
Practicing subtraction facts
   less than ten....................51

Thanksgiving
Completing a calendar 53
Dramatizing a poem 54
Matching capital and
   lowercase letters 55
Recognizing alphabetical order 59
Identifying initial consonants 60
Recognizing similarities
   and differences 61
Identifying sequence of events 62
Writing creatively..................63
Recognizing shapes 65
Completing an art project 66
Identifying number sequence........67
Identifying number values 70

Practicing addition facts
   less than thirteen 72
Practicing subtraction facts
   less than thirteen 73

Christmas
Completing a calendar 75
Dramatizing a poem 76
Matching capital and
   lowercase letters 77
Recognizing rhyming words 81
Recognizing similarities
   and differences 83
Identifying sequence of events 84
Making associations................85
Recognizing color words............86
Writing creatively..................87
Recognizing shapes 89
Completing an art project 90
Recognizing number sequence 91
Identifying number values 92
Practicing addition facts
   less than thirteen 94
Practicing subtraction facts
   less than thirteen 95

Valentine's Day
Completing a calendar............... 97
Dramatizing a poem 98
Listening and following directions... 99
Recognizing rhyming words.......... 101
Recognizing color words............ 102
Finding hidden words 103
Writing creatively.................. 104
Recognizing shapes 106
Completing an art project 107
Identifying number sequence 108
Recognizing number words and
   number sequence 109
Identifying number values............ 110
Practicing addition facts
   less than eighteen 111

Practicing subtraction facts
   less than eighteen 113
Completing a math project 115
Solving equations (open
   worksheets) 116

Springtime
Completing a calendar 119
Dramatizing a poem 120
Listening and following directions ... 121
Identifying initial blends 123
Finding hidden words 124
Recognizing story sequence 125
Writing creatively 126
Completing an art project 128
Recognizing number sequence 130
Identifying number sequence 131
Practicing addition facts
   less than eighteen 132
Completing a math project 133
Practicing addition facts
   less than eighteen 134
Practicing subtraction facts
   less than eighteen 135
Solving equations (open
   worksheets 137

Teacher Guide

Introduction

The Big Fearon Book of Teachers' Holiday Helpers provides busy teachers with high-quality, easy-to-prepare lessons for the primary classroom. The charming characters on the activity pages and the easy-to-make bulletin board displays generate anticipation for seasonal events. In this book you will find everything you need to provide practice in essential skills and to develop students' enthusiasm.

In the section Bulletin Board Displays, sample bulletin board designs, patterns, and instructions are given for instant bulletin board success throughout the year. You can follow the instructions to prepare duplicates of the sample designs, or you might choose to reproduce the patterns and create your own designs. In combination with the children's activity sheets from this book, or as separate decorative displays, the bulletin boards are sure to be highlights in your classroom.

The first two activities for each holiday or season are designed to develop your students' interest. For each month, you may want to begin by using the calendar to show students several events within the month. Then, dramatizing finger plays will develop students' listening and language skills and will introduce them to the characters that appear on the activity pages.

In this book, there are over one hundred additional activity sheets to help you develop students' skills in reading, math, creative writing, and art. Each reproducible worksheet is accented with delightful characters for your students to color. For Valentine's Day and Springtime, the final activity sheets are open worksheets that are designed for flexibility in planning additional practice in addition and subtraction. Write your choice of math problems in the workspaces and the answers at the bottom of the pages. Students can then add, subtract, and check their answers as directed.

For your convenience, all the poems, puppet-making instructions, and guidelines for dramatic puppetry are located in one section, Calendar and Finger Play Guide, beginning on page 27.

Bulletin Board Displays

Halloween

Thanksgiving

Christmas

Valentine's Day

• 3

Springtime

You may copy or enlarge the bulletin board patterns according to the proportions that are determined by the size of your bulletin board space. You may wish to make more than one tracing of the patterns in different sizes for use in several places in your classroom. Tracings can be made by using either an opaque or overhead projector. You can trace the images onto a white surface and then color them with crayons, pastels, or paints. Or you might trace selected parts of the characters (hair, eyes, clothing) onto sheets of colored construction paper and overlay them on the final images.

To make a tracing using an opaque projector, simply place the pattern in the projector and focus the projection on a sheet of paper or tagboard that is sized according to your needs. Then trace the image. To make a tracing using an overhead projector, make a transparency of the pattern and place the transparency on the projector. Focus the image and trace it onto your paper or tagboard.

Basic Steps
To make the bulletin board displays, follow these simple steps:
1. Reproduce the bulletin board patterns for your display. Adjust their sizes to the area of your bulletin board. (If you want to add different textures to the characters, see the section "Extra Textures.")

2. Cover the bulletin board with construction paper.
3. See the next section for directions to make the scenic parts of your display.
4. Staple or pin the separate pieces into place.

Scenic Parts

fence: Cut out strips from brown construction paper, wood-grain Con-Tact paper, or cardboard. Arrange and staple the strips to form a fence.

leaves: Collect and then staple real leaves to the board. Or cut out leaf shapes from red, yellow, green, and orange tissue paper.

moon: Cut out a large circle from yellow construction paper. To make a sparkling moon, spray the circle with aerosol glue and then sprinkle it lightly with gold or silver glitter.

trees: Tear one or more sheets of black paper to form the shape of a tree. You may want to sketch the tree first and then tear along the lines of your sketch.

buds: Use small wads of green tissue or crepe paper. Staple them along the tips of the branches.

weeds: Cut out pointed strips of green and tan construction paper. Group the strips to make the effect of clustered weeds.

Extra Textures
Halloween:

witch: Add texture to the hair with strips of colored crepe paper. Glue strips of yarn on the shoes for shoelaces. Attach bright buttons to the dress. Glue lace to the collar and cuffs. Glue on a colorful ribbon for the hatband.

bat: Pleat darkly colored tissue paper and paste it over the wings. Make the eyes out of white and black construction paper.

ghost: Make the tongue out of red construction paper and the eyes from orange and yellow construction paper. For a sparkling ghost, spray with aerosol glue and sprinkle lightly with glitter.

skeleton: Trace the bones on textured wallpaper. Add a big red heart behind the ribs.

cat: Make the whiskers out of pipe cleaners. Use a pompon of colorful yarn for the nose.

Thanksgiving:

Pilgrim: Add texture to the hair with strips of colored crepe paper. Attach metal belt buckles for the belt, hat, or shoes.

Indian: Make the hair by braiding yarn into large braids. Glue colorful beads, sequins, or rickrack to trim the headband, clothes, or shoes. To add fringe to the clothes, cut out and clip the edges of strips of crepe paper. Staple these fringed strips along the outside edges of the arms and legs.

turkey: Trace the turkey body on brown paper. Use brightly colored tissue for the feathers and orange paper for the feet. Attach a deflated red balloon for the wattle.

mouse: Add pipe cleaners for the whiskers. Use a pompon of brightly colored yarn for the nose.

Christmas:

tree: For a sparkling tree, spray the tree with aerosol glue and sprinkle lightly with green glitter. Decorate the tree with ornaments made by the children. Attach ready-made ornaments, pompon balls, candy canes, or garland.

Santa: Glue on cotton for the hair, beard, cuffs, hat, and coat trim. Attach a metal belt buckle to Santa's belt.

sitting elf: Add strips of crepe paper for the hair. Glue on cotton for the trim on the hat. Glue brightly colored tissue paper on the light bulbs.

standing elf: Add strips of yarn to texture the hair. Glue on cotton to trim the hat. Use brightly colored wrapping paper and ribbon to cover the gift box. Use string to attach little bells to the tips on the elf's shoes.

Valentine's Day:

balloons: Use sheets of tissue paper for the balloons. Attach colorful yarn for the strings. Make the bow from brightly colored ribbon.

bear: Trace the bear onto felt or fuzzy paper. Use a yarn pompon for the nose.

penguin: Put a cloth scarf around the penguin's neck.

dog: Trace the dog onto felt or fuzzy paper. Attach a yarn pompon for the nose. Use a real dog collar, or make the dog's collar from a piece of colorful ribbon. Decorate the ribbon with sequins, beads, or glitter.

Springtime:

bunny: Glue cotton on the tail for a fluffy effect. Attach a yarn pompon for the nose. Use pipe cleaners for the whiskers.

duck: Trace the raincoat onto patterned wallpaper. Trace the hat, boots, and umbrella onto vinyl Con-Tact paper. Staple the umbrella to the bulletin board over crumpled paper to make it three dimensional.

cloud, sun, and rainbow: Spray the sun lightly with aerosol glue and lightly sprinkle it with glitter. Spray the cloud with white "snowflake" spray and then sprinkle with glitter. Use brightly colored tissue paper for the rainbow.

Halloween

Bulletin board pattern • 7

8 • Bulletin board pattern

Halloween

Halloween

Bulletin board pattern • 9

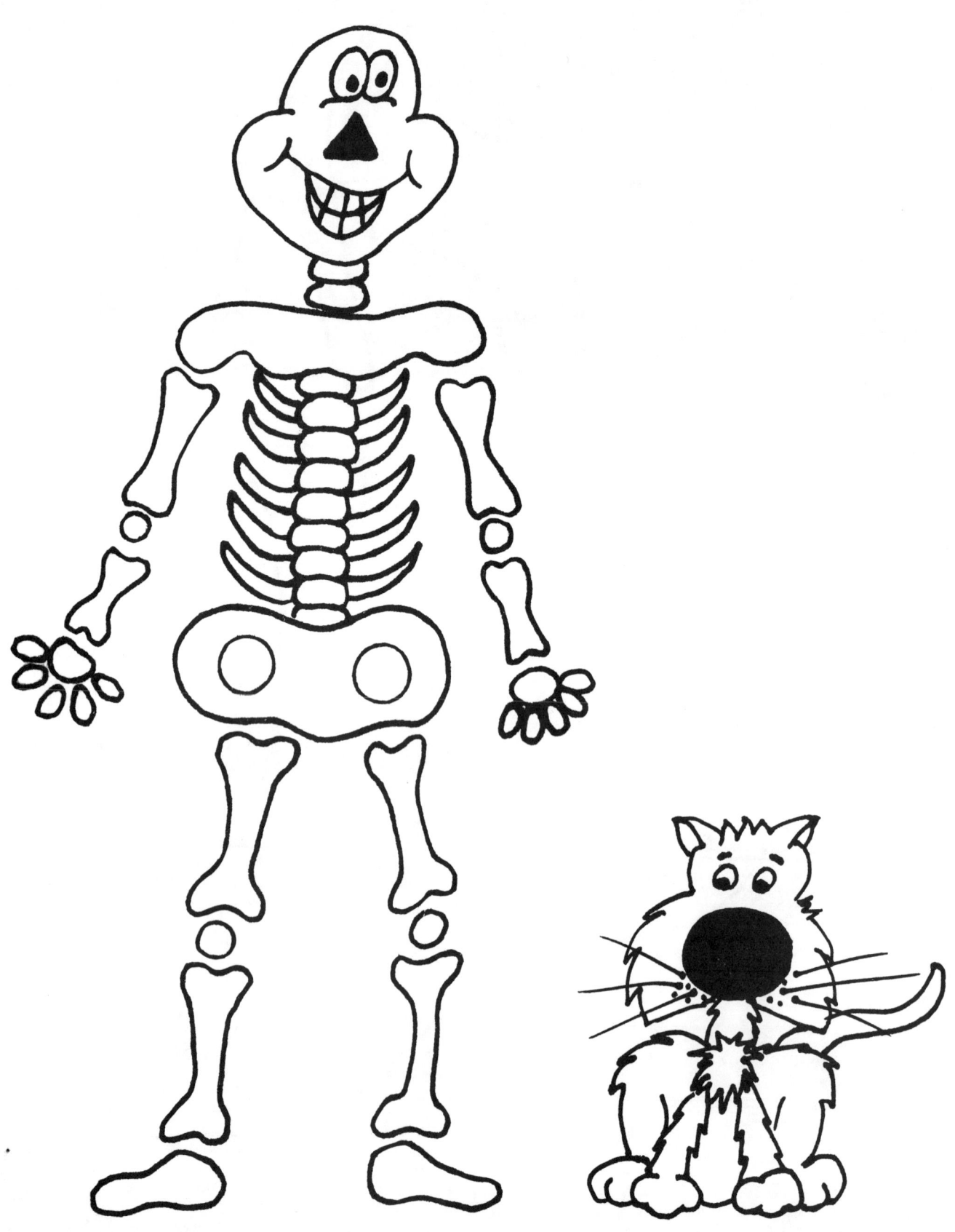

10 • Bulletin board patterns

Halloween

Thanksgiving

Bulletin board pattern • 11

12 • Bulletin board pattern

Thanksgiving

Christmas

Bulletin board pattern • 15

16 • Bulletin board pattern

Christmas

Christmas Bulletin board pattern • 17

18 • Bulletin board pattern

Christmas

20 • Bulletin board pattern

Valentine's Day

Valentine's Day Bulletin board pattern • 21

Springtime

Bulletin board pattern • 25

26 • Bulletin board pattern

Springtime

Calendar and Finger Play Guide

Calendar Activities

The calendars may be completed to help orient the children to the events of each month. Reproduce enough calendars to provide one for each child and one for demonstration each time you present a calendar lesson. Direct the children to trace or write the name of the month and show them where to write the numbers that represent the dates. Discuss the date of each holiday with respect to other events, for example, school holidays and children's birthdays. Children will learn from these orientations, and their anticipation will increase as you use the other seasonal activities in this book.

Dramatization with Finger Puppets

Plan to provide each child with one or two finger puppets. Reproduce the puppet patterns onto heavy paper or lightweight cardboard. For the October and November puppets, you may want to cut the puppets apart and cut out the finger holes before distributing the puppets to the children. Then for all months, have the children color and cut out their puppets.

Discuss several aspects of finger puppetry: listening, moving puppets at appropriate times, speaking clearly, and so on. For each finger play lesson, read the poem to the children. Discuss each character and its actions. Discuss the ways the children might move their puppets. Allow the children to practice reciting each stanza of the poem and moving or resting their puppets appropriately before they dramatize the entire poem. Additional suggestions for individual finger plays are provided with each poem below.

Halloween, page 32: Each child should have one or two puppets.

On Halloween Night

On Halloween night,
You'll see such a sight,
As a witch who's out riding her broom.

Just watch the old bones,
As they dance on their toes,
By the light of the Halloween moon.

And if you look hard,
You'll see in the yard,
A ghost floating around in the breeze.

Oh! Don't miss the bat,
With the floppy old hat,
As he darts in and out of the trees.

You will see this and more,
When you look out your door.
It's the great costume night, Halloween!

Thanksgiving, page 54: For puppetry, each child should have one or two puppets. To use the body movements, demonstrate the motions described below and discuss the appropriate times to perform them. Practice one stanza at a time.

Five Little Turkeys   *to dramatize

Five little turkeys
went outside to play.
Mother said, "Be careful!
It's Thanksgiving Day!"

The first little turkey   *(Have the children put a hand
Didn't even see   above their eyes and pretend
The Indian who was hiding   to look for Indians.)
Behind the maple tree.

The second little turkey   *(Have the children stamp their
Decided she'd better scoot   feet for the sound of the boots.
When she heard the sound   Then have them run in place as
Of the little Pilgrim's boots.   the turkey runs away.)

The third little turkey   *(Have the children pretend to
Went to climb a tree.   climb a tree and then fall to
He climbed too high   the floor.)
And fell and skinned his knee.

The fourth little turkey   *(Have the children put their
Didn't have a care.   hands on their hips and sway
She went running in the woods   back and forth. Then have
And she saw a Pilgrim there.   them run in place.)

The fifth little turkey   *(Have the children look around
Was left all alone.   for other turkeys. Then have
He started to cry   them pretend to cry and run in
And ran all the way home.   place.)

Christmas, page 76: Each child should have one or two puppets. Completed puppets can be taped to drinking staws or strips of lightweight cardboard. The poem can be recited, or it can be sung to the tune of "The Twelve Days of Christmas."

Santa Saves the Elves

Mrs. Claus told Santa,
"You know it's Christmas Eve!
The elves have been so busy,
Are you packed and ready?
You know, it's almost time for you to leave!"

The first little elf
Was sent to trim the tree.
The light got strung around him,
That's how Santa found him,
So, Santa had to set the elf free.

The second little elf
Was sent to tie the bows.
The ribbon wrapped around him,
That's how Santa found him,
So, Santa had to set the elf free.

The third little elf
Was sent to hitch the team.
A reindeer sat upon him,
That's how Santa found him,
So, Santa had to set the elf free.

The fourth little elf
Was sent to pack the sleigh.
The toy bag fell upon him,
That's how Santa found him,
So, Santa had to set the elf free.

The fifth little elf
Was sent for Santa's list.
The list got wound around him,
That's how Santa found him,
So, Santa had to set the elf free.

Valentine's Day, page 98: Each child should have two or three finger puppets (one or two characters and one blank heart puppet as the Valentine for their secret friend). Puppets can be taped to drinking straws or strips of cardboard.

A Valentine's Day Poem

Friends are very special
That's why I chose today,
To send each one a Valentine
That I made a special way.

The first one went to a puppy
Who doesn't have a name,
I only got her yesterday
But I love her just the same.

The second one went to a bunny
Who lives inside his hutch,
I feed him all the vegetables
That my mom gives me for lunch.

The third one went to a panda
Who promised me to keep,
All the secrets that we'd shared
Before we fell asleep.

The fourth one went to a turtle
Who lives inside her shell,
I'd like to take her for a walk,
But she doesn't move too well.

The fifth one went to someone
That only I can tell,
We play together all day long;
We know each other well.

Springtime, page 120: Direct the children to fold their puppet patterns on the dotted lines and to apply paste in the space marked *paste here*. Then direct them to paste together the two areas that have been folded back on the dotted lines. Discuss how the puppet might be turned to face the audience as the poem tells of the bunny's ailment and recuperation.

The Little Bunny Is Sick

OH, NO!

The little bunny is sick,
He thinks he has the flu.
He can't get out of bed,
And there's still so much to do!

He's going to need some helpers,
But he's not sure just who.
Could *you* help the little bunny?
Would *you* know what to do?

LIKE . . .

Doing all your schoolwork,
Wiggling your ears and nose,
Eating all your carrots,
And hopping on your toes.

GUESS WHAT!

The little bunny is better,
He didn't have the flu.
He just ate too many jelly beans,
And chocolate rabbits, too!

Name _____

October

Sunday	Monday	Tuesday	Wednesday	Thursday	Friday	Saturday

Halloween

Completing a calendar • 31

Name _____

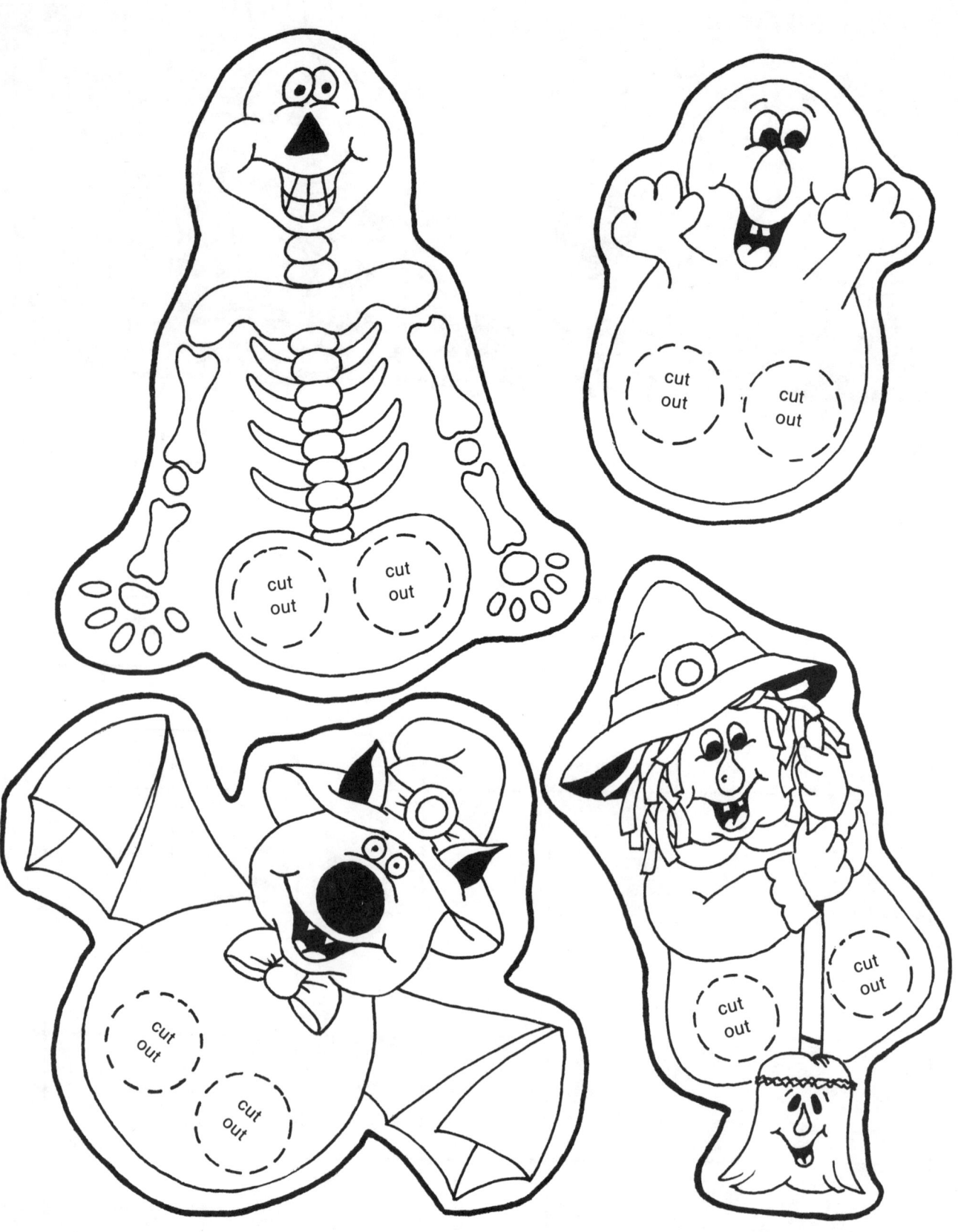

32 • Dramatizing a poem

Halloween

Name _____

Cut out and then paste the capital letters to match the lowercase letters.

h

k

l

f

r

t

| F | H | K | L | R | T |

Halloween

Matching capital and lowercase letters • 33

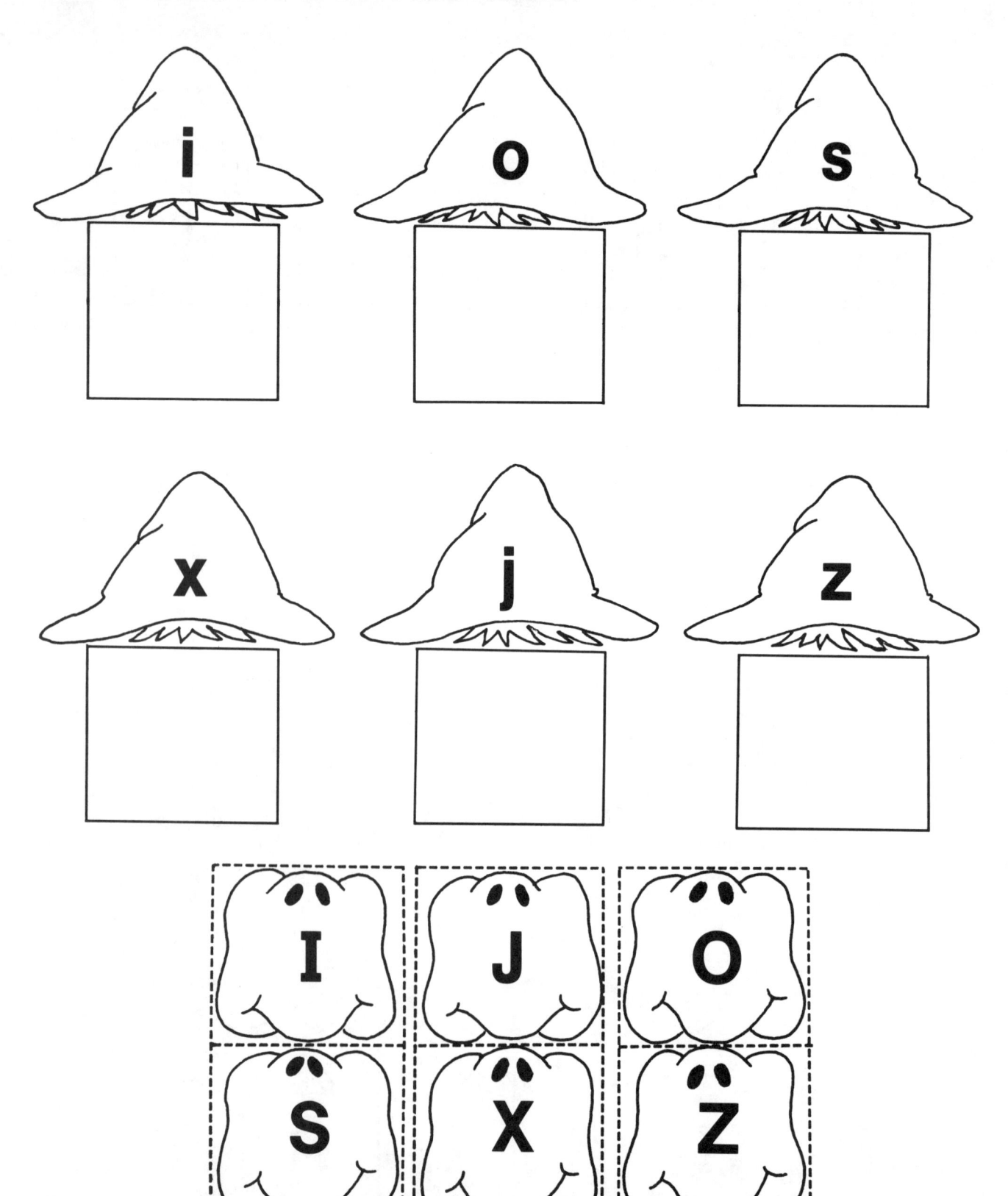

Name _____

Cut out and then paste the capital letters to match the lowercase letters.

i　　　o　　　s

x　　　j　　　z

I　J　O
S　X　Z

34 • Matching capital and lowercase letters

Halloween

Name _____

Cut out and then paste the capital letters to match the lowercase letters.

h

k

l

f

r

t

| F | H | K | L | R | T |

Halloween

Matching capital and lowercase letters • 33

Name _____

Cut out and then paste the capital letters to match the lowercase letters.

i   o   s

x   j   z

I   J   O

S   X   Z

34 • Matching capital and lowercase letters

Halloween

Name _____

Cut out and then paste the capital letters to match the lowercase letters.

n

u

w

m

v

y

| M | N | U |
| V | W | Y |

Halloween

Matching capital and lowercase letters • 35

Name _____

Cut out and then paste the capital letters to match the lowercase letters.

a   c   e   p

b   d   q   g

A   B   C   D

E   G   P   Q

36 • Matching capital and lowercase letters

Halloween

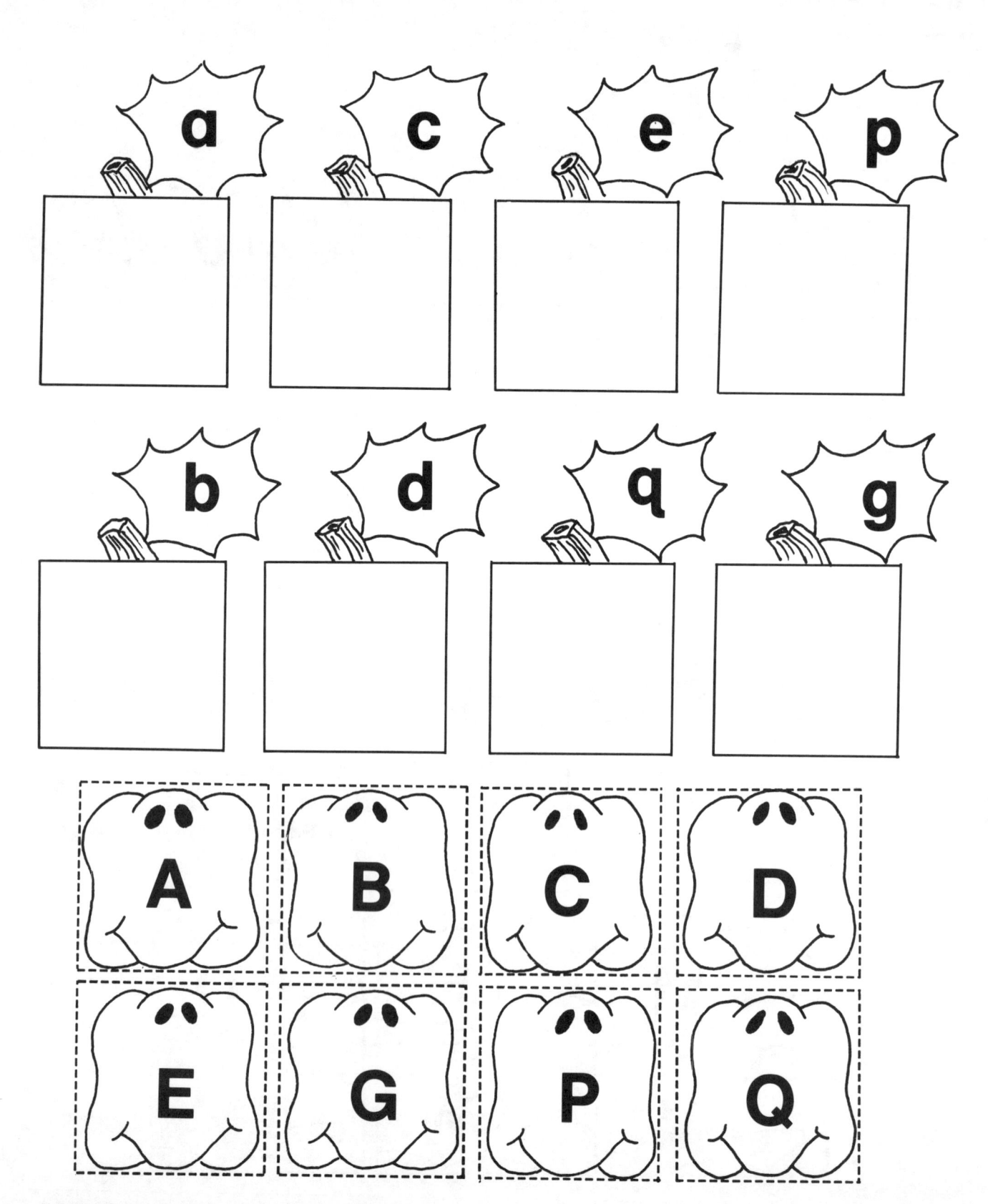

Name _____

Say the name of each picture. Circle the letter that names the beginning sound.

t p m

w r d

g t c

c t g

s z j

b k l

Halloween

Identifying initial consonants • 37

Name _____

To the teacher:
Duplicate this sheet and the next sheet on white construction paper. Help the children follow these directions to make a Halloween Spelling Spinner:

1. Color the pictures on this sheet.
2. Color the ghost and jack-o'-lantern on the other sheet. Then cut out the nose on the jack-o'-lantern.
3. Cut out the wheel on this sheet. Place it behind the jack-o'-lantern.
4. Match the dot on the wheel with the dot on the jack-o'-lantern.
5. Use a brad to attach the wheel to the jack-o'-lantern. (Push the brad through both dots.)
6. Turn the wheel.
7. Choose the vowel letters that correctly complete the words. Write the words on a separate sheet of paper.
8. Use the words in a Halloween story. Be sure to spell each word correctly.

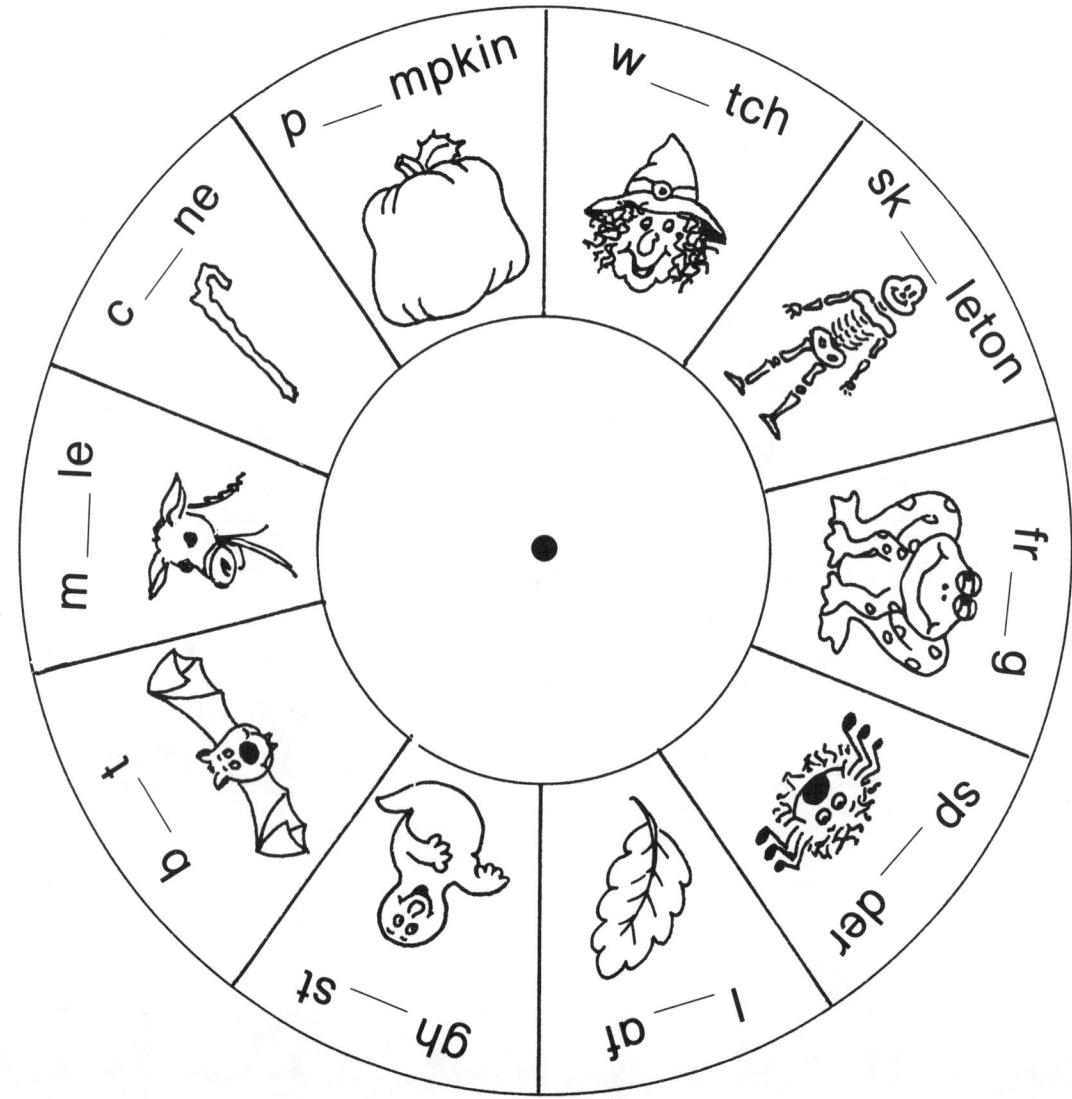

38 • Identifying missing vowel letters

Halloween

Name _____

Color the ghost and jack-o'-lantern. Cut out the nose on the jack-o'-lantern.

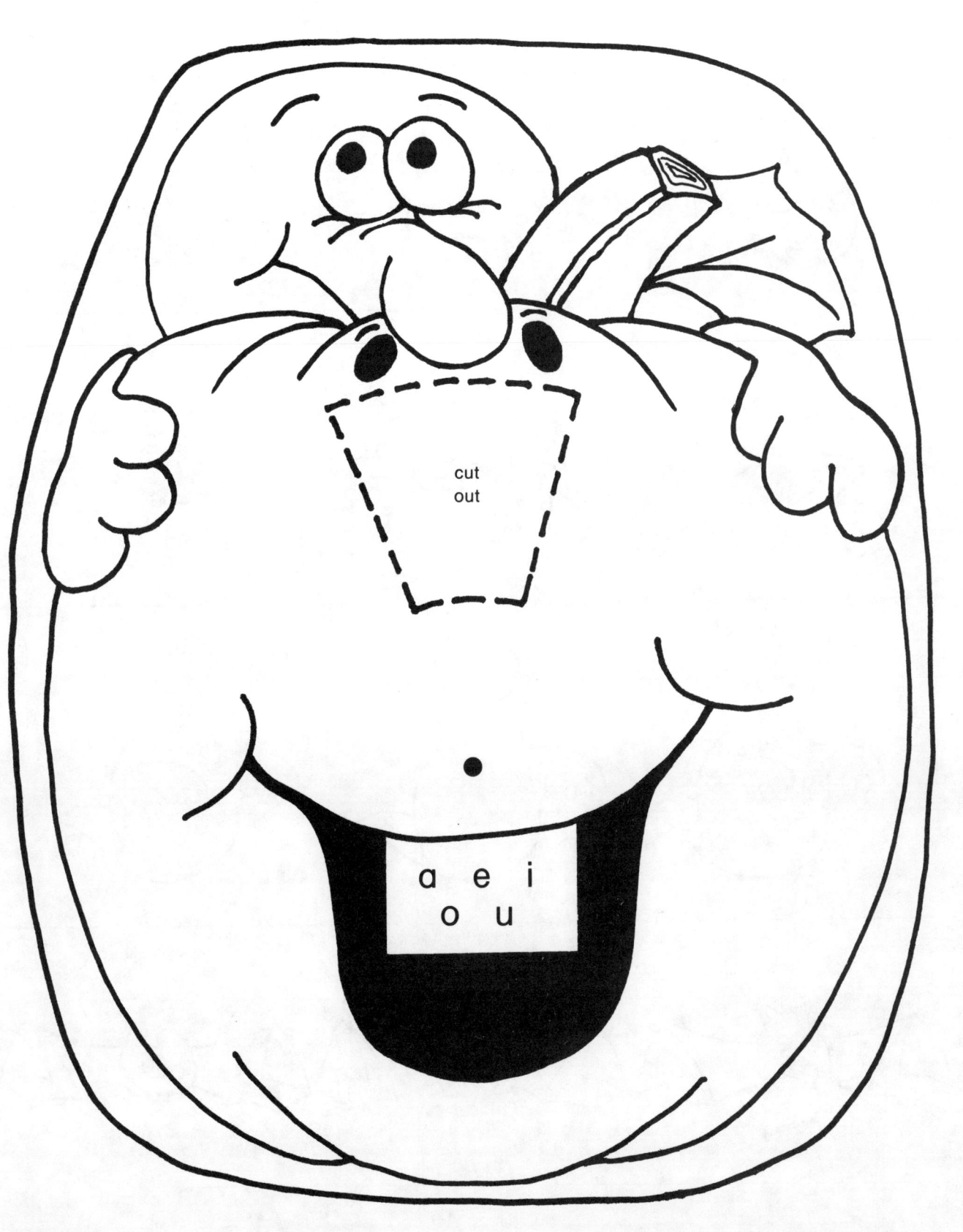

cut out

a e i
o u

Halloween Identifying missing vowel letters • 39

Name _____

For each row, color the two pictures that look alike.

40 • Recognizing similarities and differences

Halloween

Name _____

Cut out and then paste the numbers to show the correct order.

Halloween Identifying sequence of events • 41

Name _____

Cut out and then paste the correct word into each blank.

The ghost is _____ the pumpkin.

The ghost is _____ the pumpkin.

The ghost is going _____ the pumpkin.

The ghost is flying _____ the pumpkin.

| beside | into | over | under |

Using directional words

Halloween

Name _____

Write a Halloween story. Use some of the words below.

bat   happy

fun   pumpkin

ghost   witch

Halloween

Writing creatively • 43

Name _____

Use the key. Color the shapes.

KEY

△ = red
▢ = blue
▭ = yellow
◯ = green

44 • Recognizing shapes

Halloween

Name _____

Cut out and then paste the pictures to match the shapes.

Halloween

Recognizing shapes • 45

Name _____

To make the witch, do this:
Color the parts. Cut out the parts.

Paste the 🎩 on the 😀.
Paste the 👢 on the 👕.
Paste the 🧹 on the 👕.
Paste the two parts together.

paste here

paste here

paste here

paste here

46 • Completing an art project

Halloween

The Big Fearon Book of Teachers' Holiday Helpers, © 1987 David S. Lake Publishers

Name _____

For each group below, write the missing number.

5	☐	7		☐	9	10

| 6 | ☐ | 8 | | ☐ | 3 | 4 |

| 1 | 2 | ☐ | | 3 | 4 | ☐ |

Halloween   Identifying number sequence • 47

Name _____

Count the things in each set. Circle the number that tells how many.

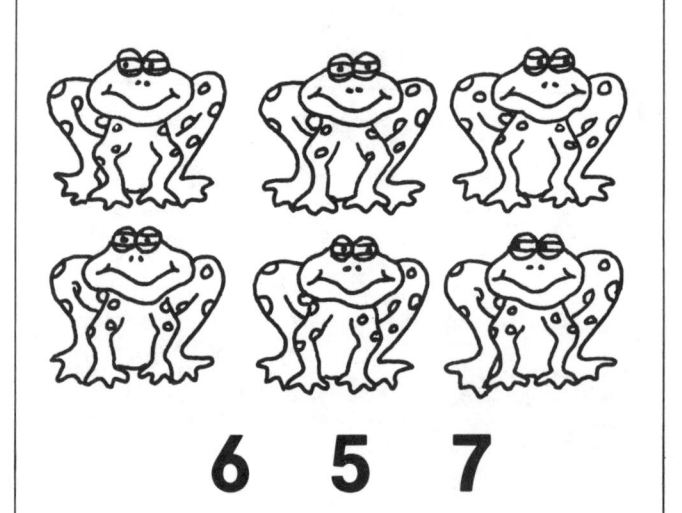

5 3 9	3 7 2
5 1 6	9 3 8
7 4 2	6 5 7

48 • Identifying number values

Halloween

Name _____

🐈 Trace the numbers.

1 2 3 4 5

6 7 8 9 10

🐈 Count the things in each set. Write the number that tells how many.

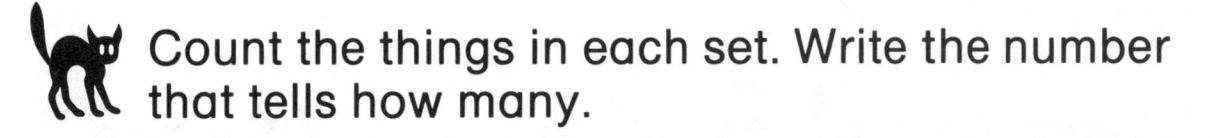

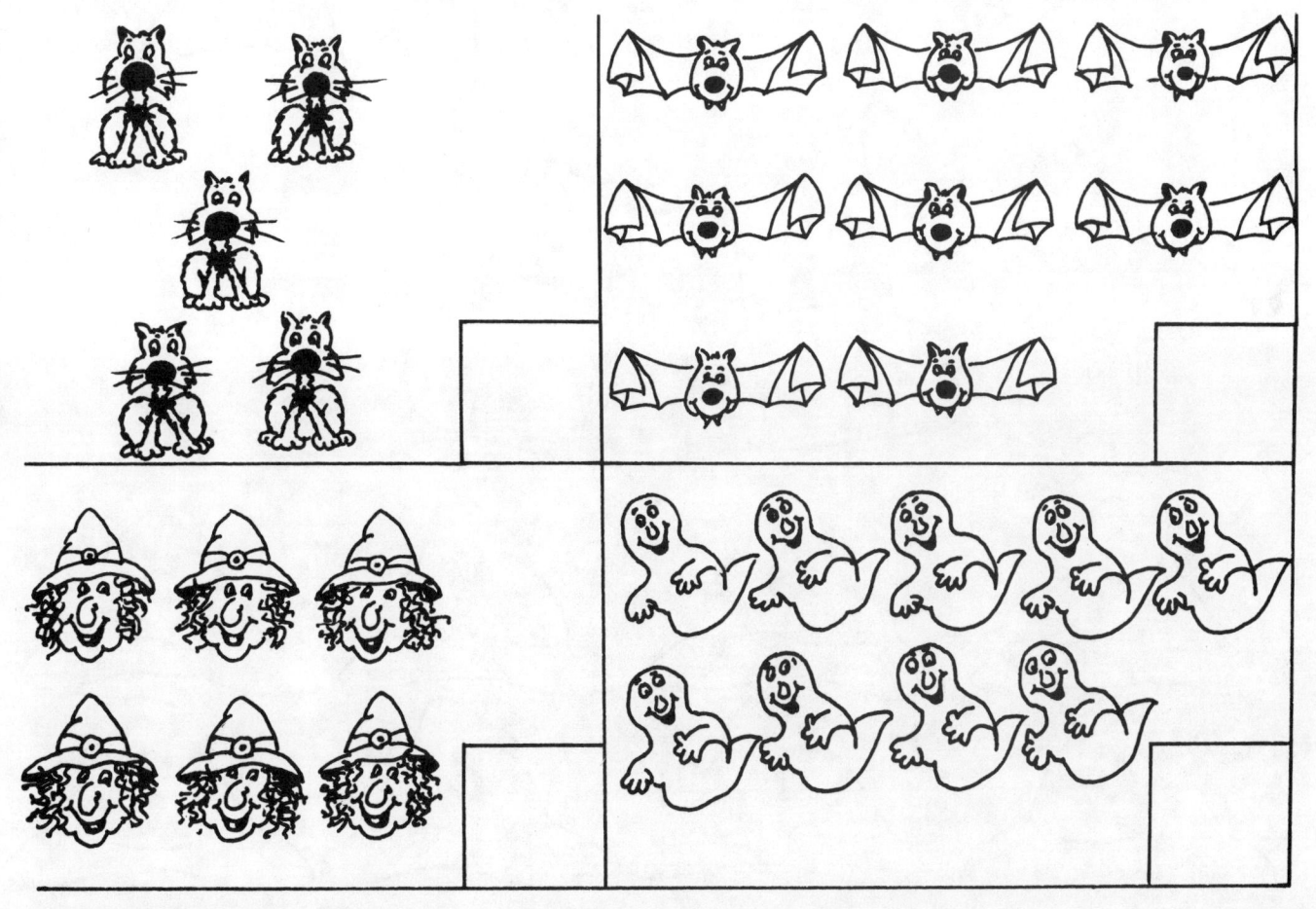

Halloween

Identifying number values • 49

Name _____

Add the numbers. Color each answer hat as you use it.

$4+3$
$5+4$
$1+2$
$1+1$
$3+3$
$6+2$
$3+2$
$2+2$

2 3 4 5
6 7 8 9

50 • Practicing addition facts less than ten

Halloween

Name _____

Subtract the numbers. Color each answer pumpkin as you use it.

9 − 3 = ☐

7 − 2 = ☐

4 − 1 = ☐

9 − 2 = ☐

8 − 4 = ☐

9 − 1 = ☐

7 − 5 = ☐

8

7

2   3   4   5   6

Halloween   Practicing subtraction facts less than ten • 51

Name _____

November

Sunday	Monday	Tuesday	Wednesday	Thursday	Friday	Saturday

Thanksgiving　　　　　　　　　　　　　　　　Completing a calendar • 53

Name _____

54 • Dramatizing a poem

Thanksgiving

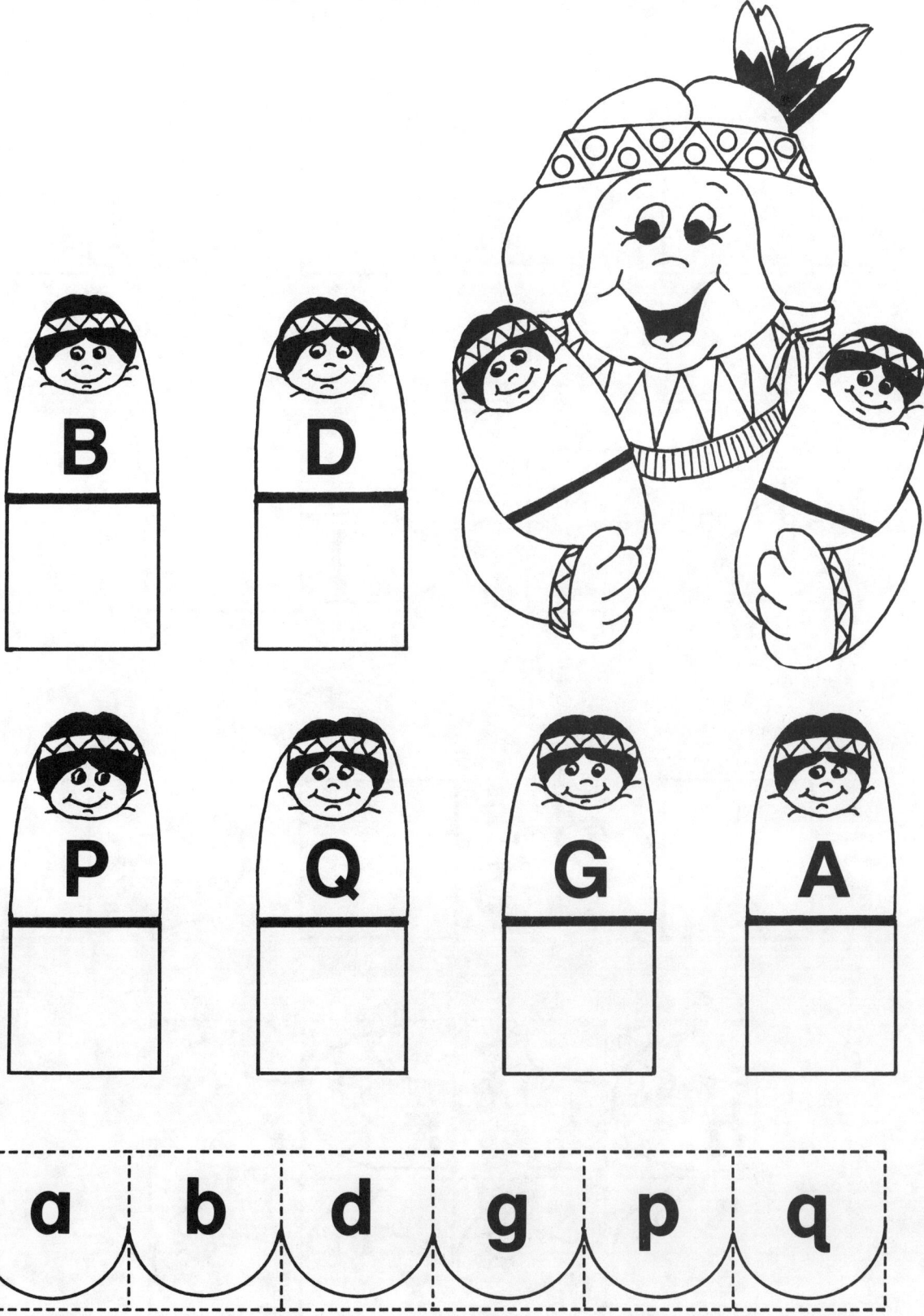

Name _____

Cut out and paste the lowercase letters to match the capital letters.

B D

P Q G A

a b d g p q

Thanksgiving Matching capital and lowercase letters • 55

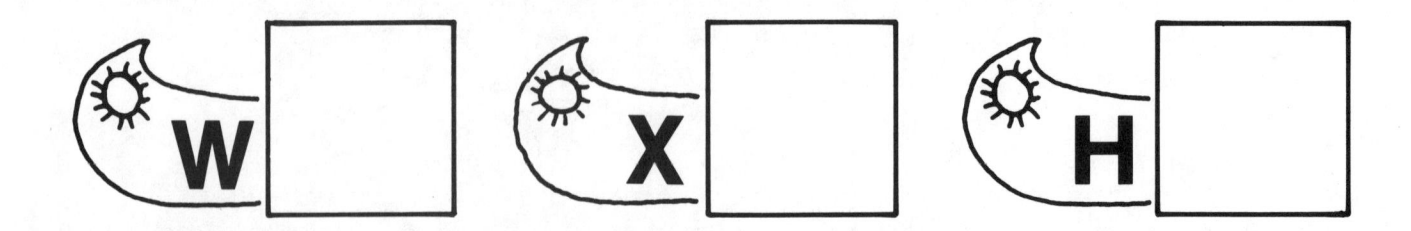

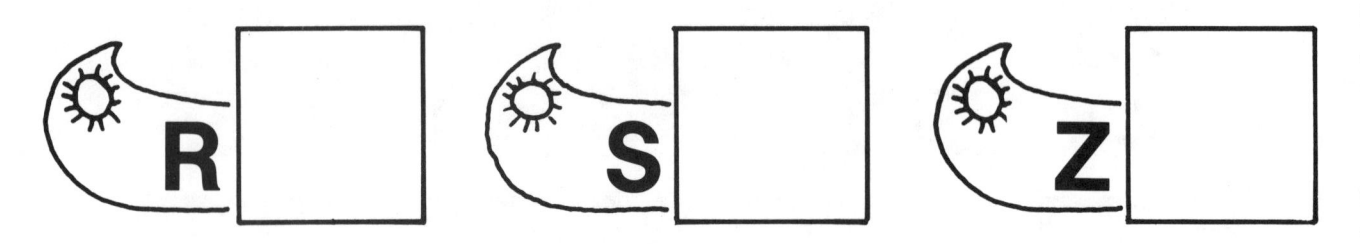

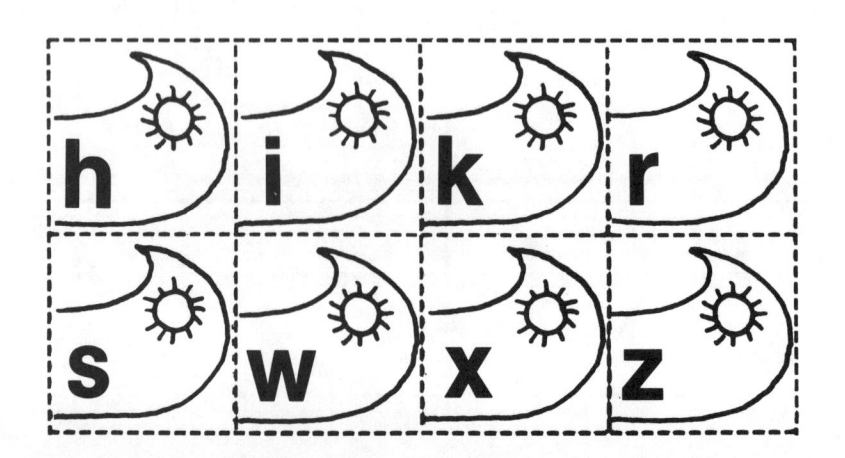

Name _____

Cut out and paste the lowercase letters to match the capital letters.

W   X   H

K   I

R   S   Z

h   i   k   r
s   w   x   z

56 • Matching capital and lowercase letters

Thanksgiving

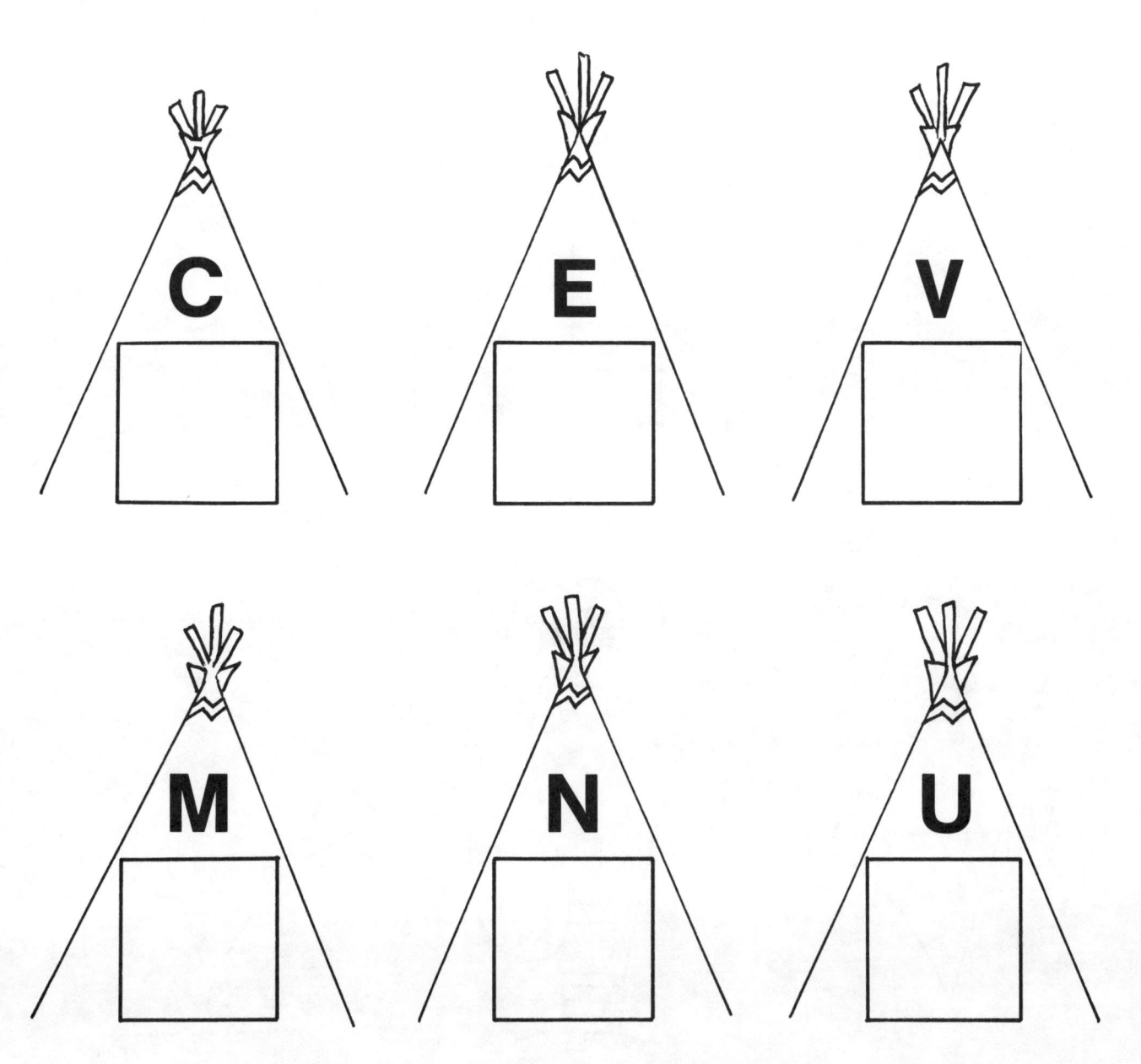

Name _____

Cut out and paste the lowercase letters to match the capital letters.

C   E   V

M   N   U

c e m n u v

Thanksgiving Matching capital and lowercase letters • 57

Name _____

Cut out and paste the lowercase letters to match the capital letters.

L Y
F T O J

f j l o t y

58 • Matching capital and lowercase letters

Thanksgiving

Name _____

🍁 Connect the dots in ABC order.

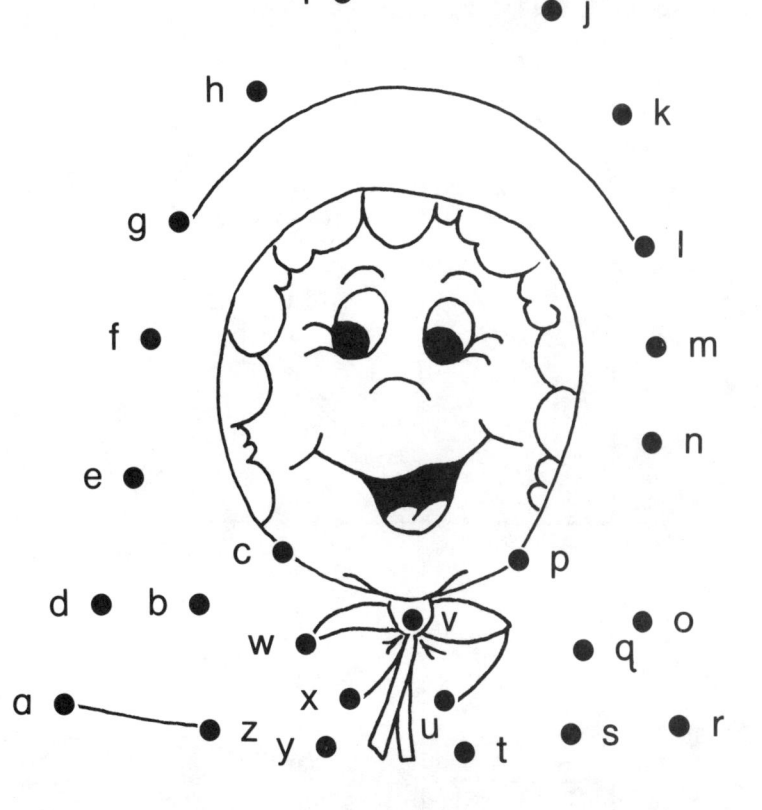

🍁 Trace the letters. Write the missing letters.

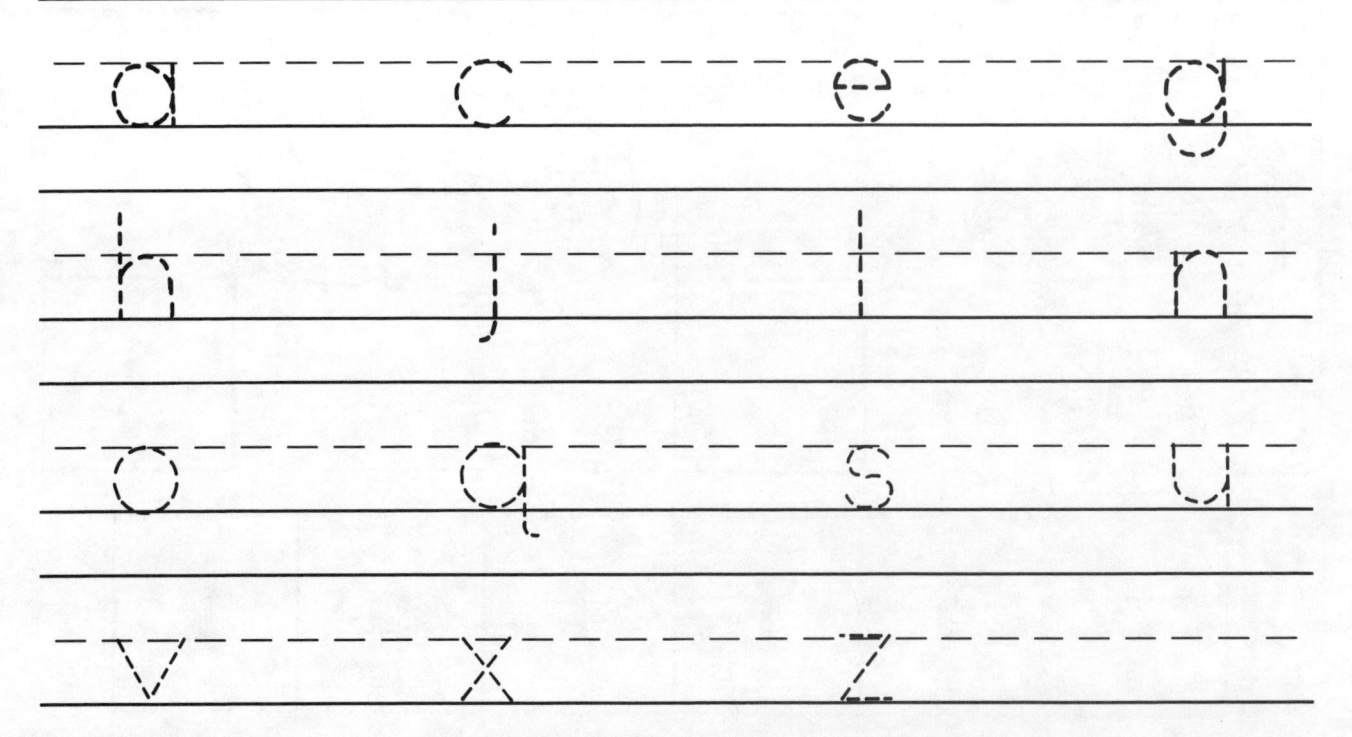

a   c   e   g

h   j   l   n

o   q   s   u

v   x   z

Thanksgiving

Recognizing alphabetical order • 59

Name _____

Cut out and then paste the beginning sound letters for the pictures.

| b | c | f | l | p | t |

60 • Identifying initial consonants

Thanksgiving

Name _____

In each row, color the two pictures that look alike.

Thanksgiving   Recognizing similarities and differences • 61

Name _____

Cut out and then paste the numbers to show the correct order.

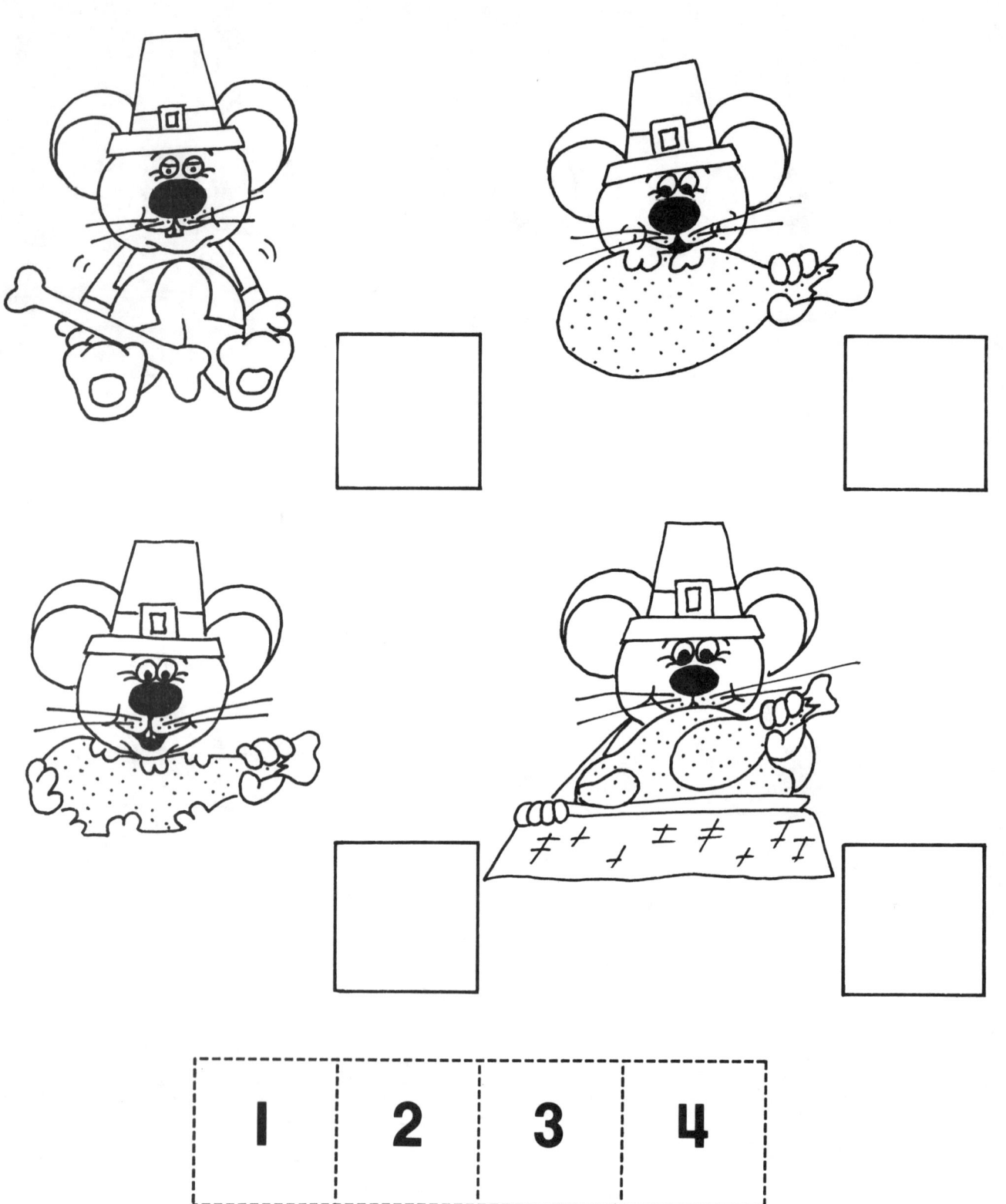

| 1 | 2 | 3 | 4 |

62 • Identifying sequence of events

Thanksgiving

Name _____

Write a Thanksgiving story. Use some of the words below.

dinner   Pilgrim

happy   sharing

Indian   turkey

Thanksgiving Writing creatively • 63

Name _____

Write a letter to invite someone to share your Thanksgiving feast.

Name _____

Use the key. Color the shapes.

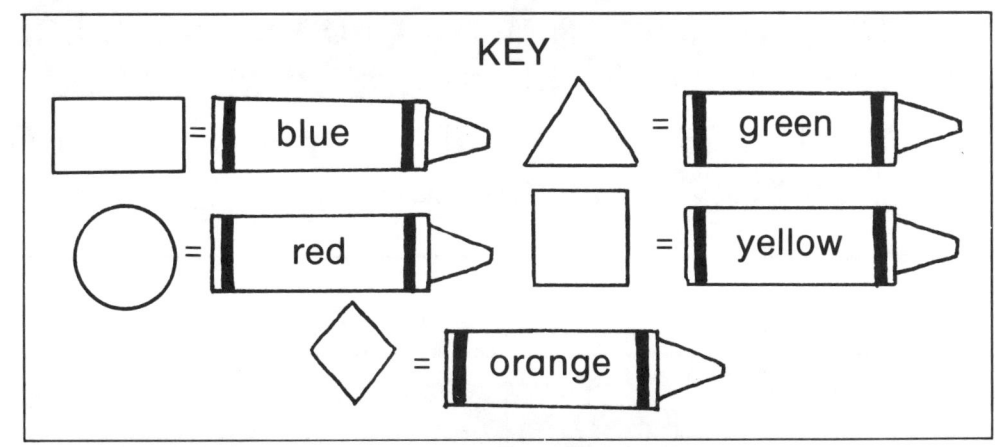

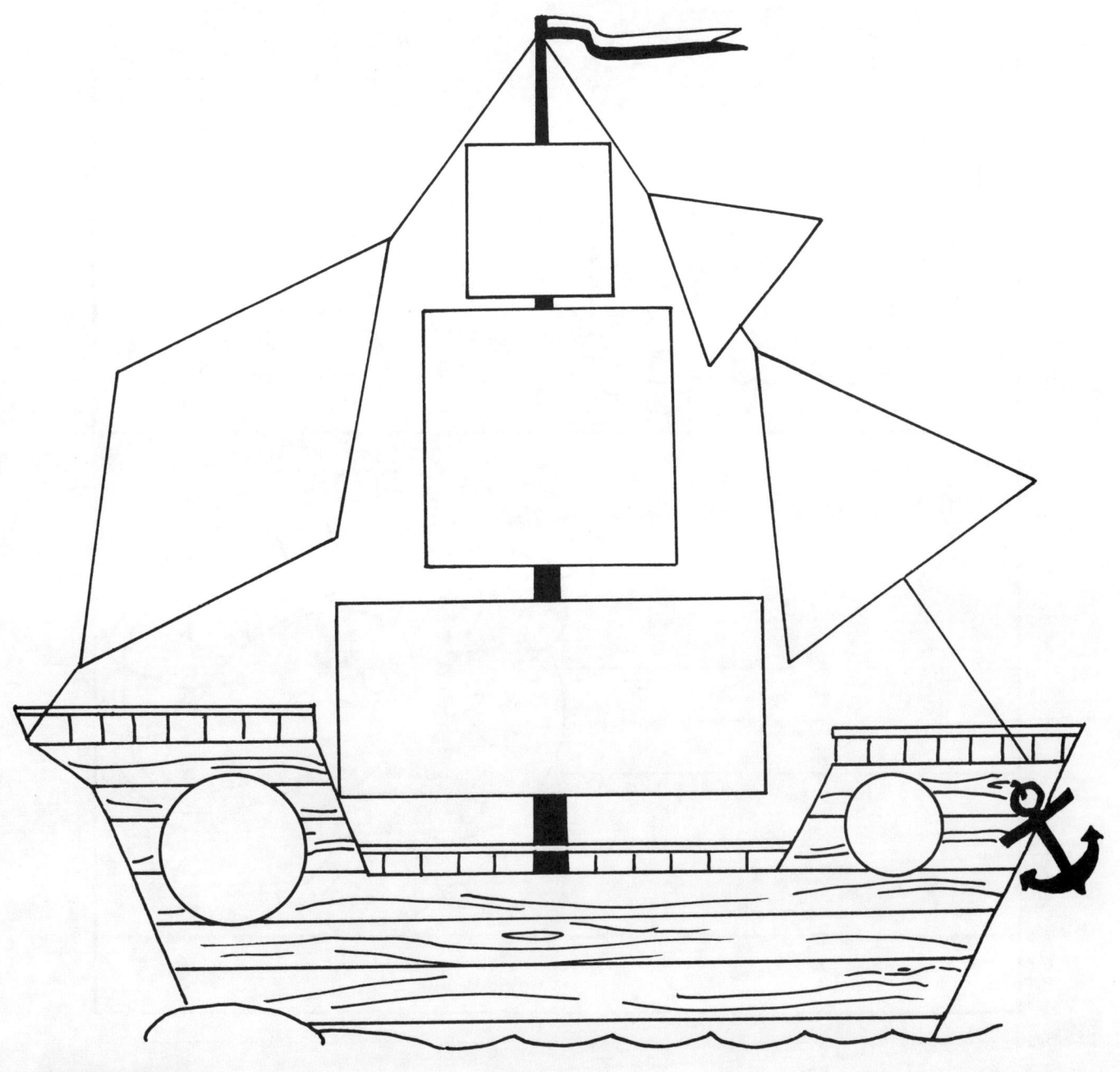

KEY

☐ = blue   △ = green

◯ = red   □ = yellow

◇ = orange

Thanksgiving   Recognizing shapes • 65

Name _____

To make a Thanksgiving name card, do this: Color the pictures. Print your name on the lines. Cut out the card. Fold the card on the dotted lines. Stand your name card on your desk or at your Thanksgiving dinner table.

66 • Completing an art project

Thanksgiving

Name _____

🍁 Cut out the baby turkeys at the bottom of the page. Then paste them in correct counting order.

1

9

7 5 10 6
8 2 4 3

Thanksgiving

Identifying number sequence • 67

Name _____

Cut out the baby turkeys at the bottom of the page. Then paste them in correct counting order.

68 • Identifying number sequence

Thanksgiving

Name _____

For each group, write the missing number.

☐ 11 12

16 17 ☐

12 ☐ 14

13 14 ☐

☐ 18 19

18 ☐ 20

Thanksgiving

Identifying number sequence • 69

Name _____

Count the things in each set. Circle the number that tells how many.

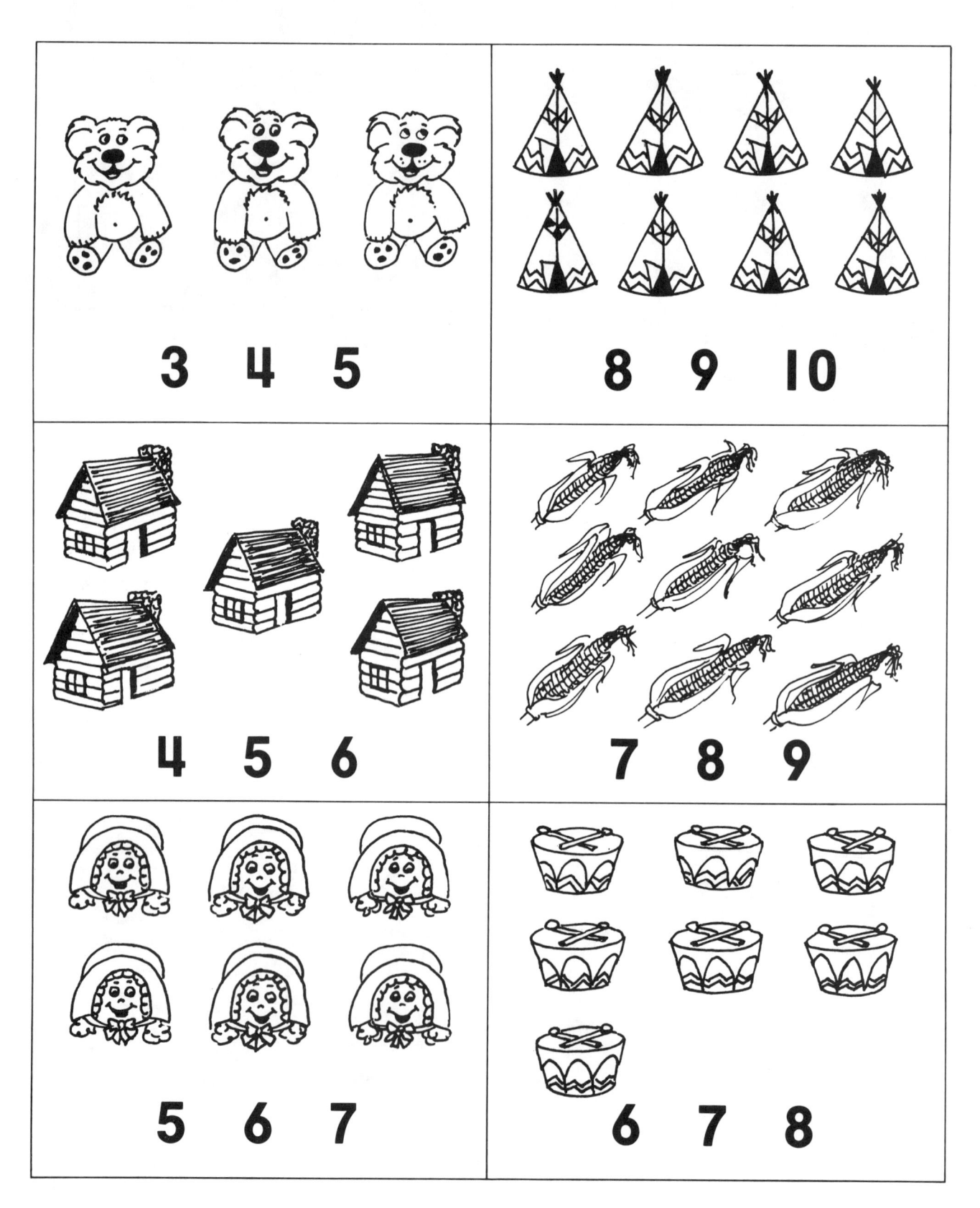

3 4 5	8 9 10
4 5 6	7 8 9
5 6 7	6 7 8

70 • Identifying number values

Thanksgiving

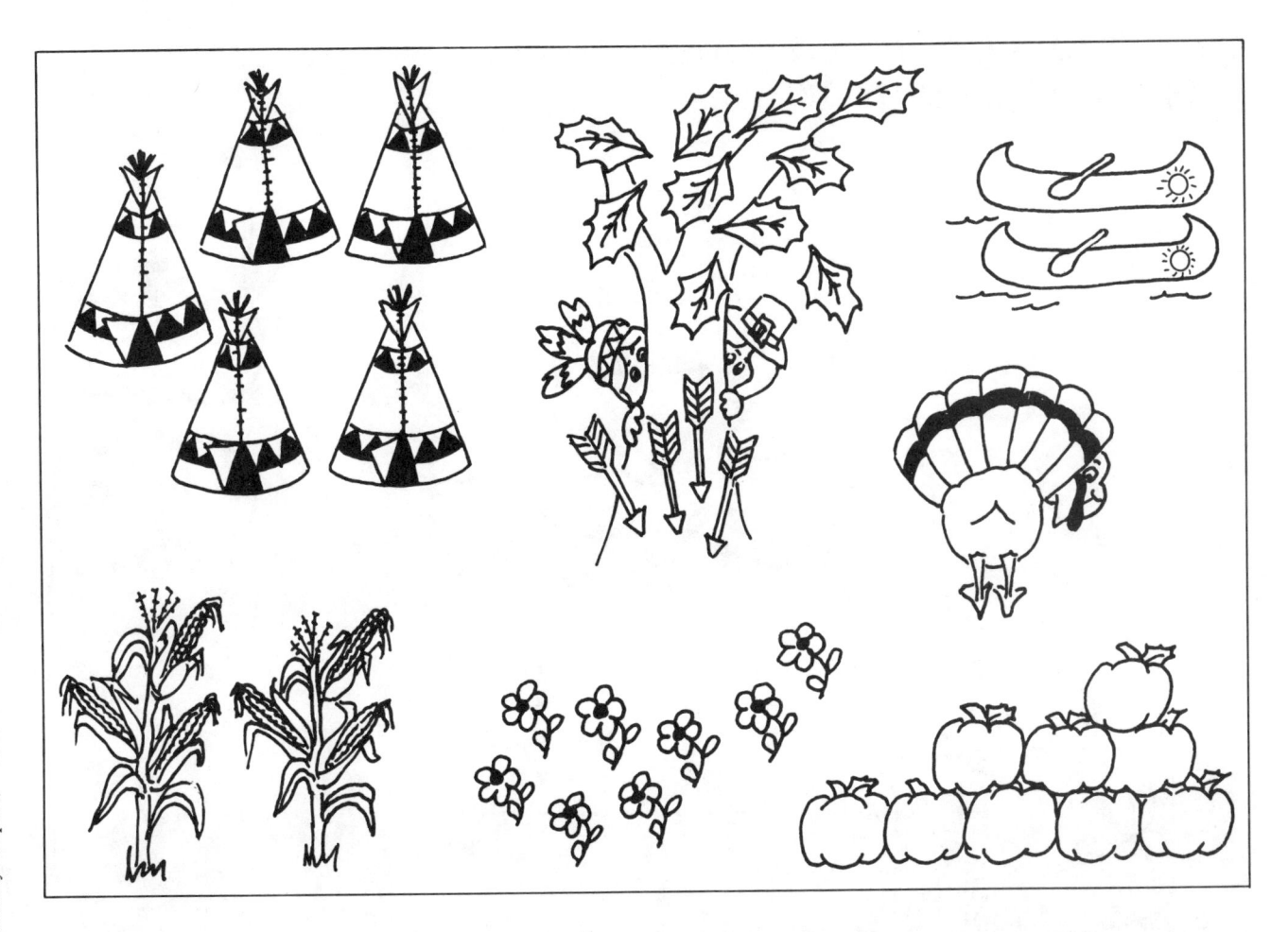

Name _____

Count the things in the picture above. Write the numbers that tell how many.

How many 🏹 ?

How many 🌸 ?

How many ⛺ ?

How many 🍁 ?

How many 🌽 ?

How many 🎃 ?

How many 🌽 ?

How many 🦃 ?

How many 🛶 ?

How many 🎩 ?

Thanksgiving

Identifying number values • 71

Name _____

Add the numbers. Color each answer pumpkin as you use it.

6   8
+4   +3

1   5   2
+4   +7   +5

4   4   7
+2   +4   +2

7
8
9
10
11
12
5
6

72 • Practicing addition facts less than thirteen

Thanksgiving

Name _____

Subtract the numbers. Color each answer turkey as you use it.

12 − 6 = ☐
11 − 1 = ☐
10 − 7 = ☐
11 − 6 = ☐
10 − 2 = ☐
9 − 5 = ☐
12 − 3 = ☐
9 − 2 = ☐

Thanksgiving

Practicing subtraction facts less than thirteen • 73

Name _____

Sunday	Monday	Tuesday	Wednesday	Thursday	Friday	Saturday

Christmas

Completing a calendar • 75

Name _____

76 • Dramatizing a poem

Christmas

Name _____

Cut out and paste the lowercase letters to match the capital letters.

G   M   N

J   C   A

a   c   j   g   m   n

Christmas

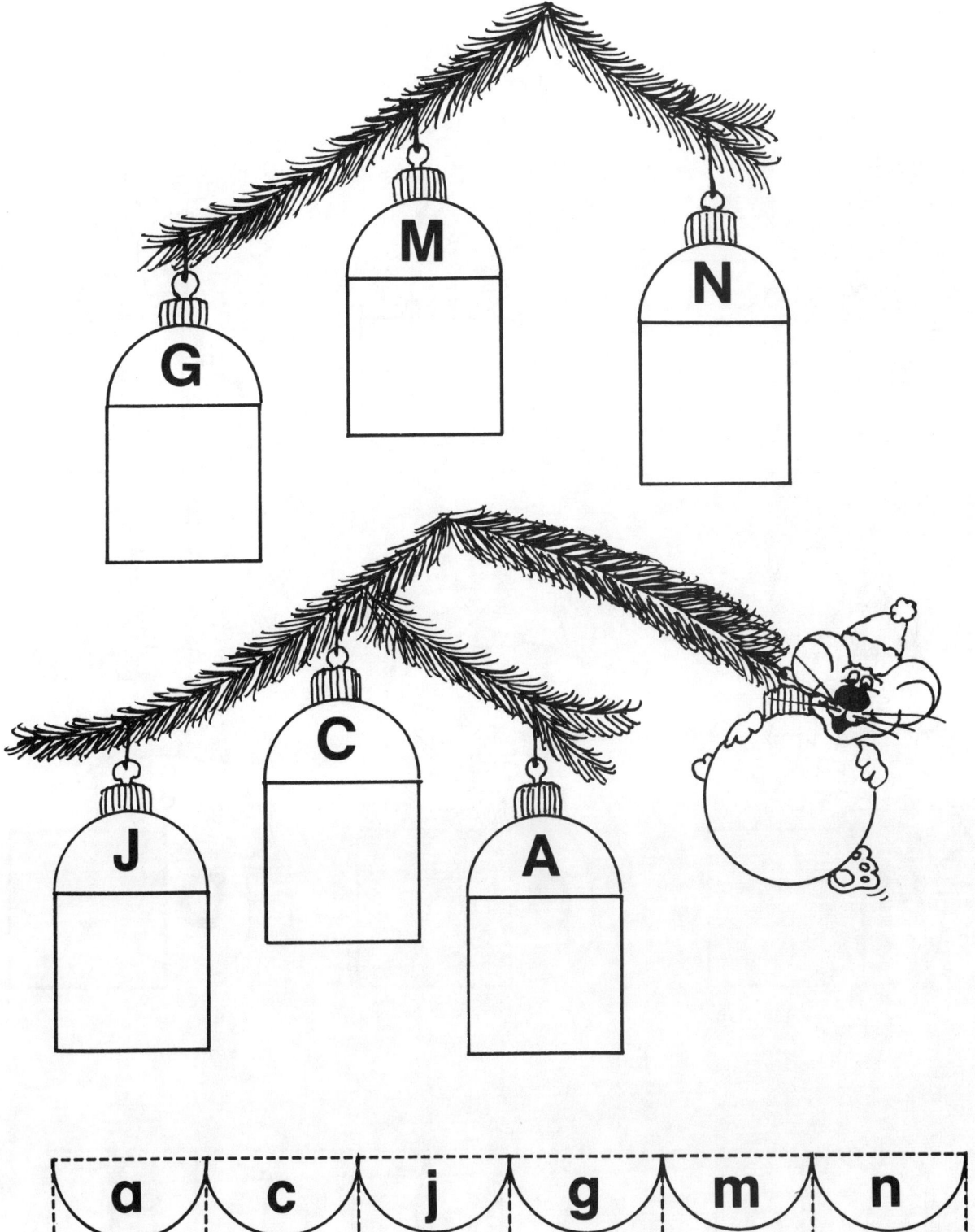

Matching capital and lowercase letters • 77

Name _____

Cut out and paste the lowercase letters to match the capital letters.

F　T　K

H　B　D

b　d　f　h　k　t

78 • Matching capital and lowercase letters

Christmas

Name _____

Cut out and paste the lowercase letters to match the capital letters.

O

L

P

Q

E

I

| e | i | l | o | p | q |

Christmas　　　　　　　　　　　　　　Matching capital and lowercase letters • 79

Name _____

Cut out and paste the lowercase letters to match the capital letters.

S   Z   X

U   V

R   W   Y

r	s	u	v
w	x	y	z

80 • Matching capital and lowercase letters

Christmas

Name _____

To the teacher:

Duplicate this sheet and the next sheet on white construction paper. Help the children follow these directions to make a Holiday Rhyming-Word Spinner:
1. Color all the pictures on this sheet.
2. Cut out the pictures at the bottom of this sheet. Match and then paste the pictures to make pairs of rhyming words on the wheel.
3. Color the picture of Santa Claus on the other sheet. Then cut out the rectangle on the front of Santa.
4. Cut out the wheel on this sheet. Place it behind Santa.
5. Match the dot on the wheel with the dot on Santa's buckle.
6. Use a brad to attach the wheel to Santa. (Push the brad through both dots.)
7. Turn the wheel. Say the rhyming words.
8. Use as many words as you can to write a little poem on another sheet of paper. Be sure to spell the rhyming words correctly.

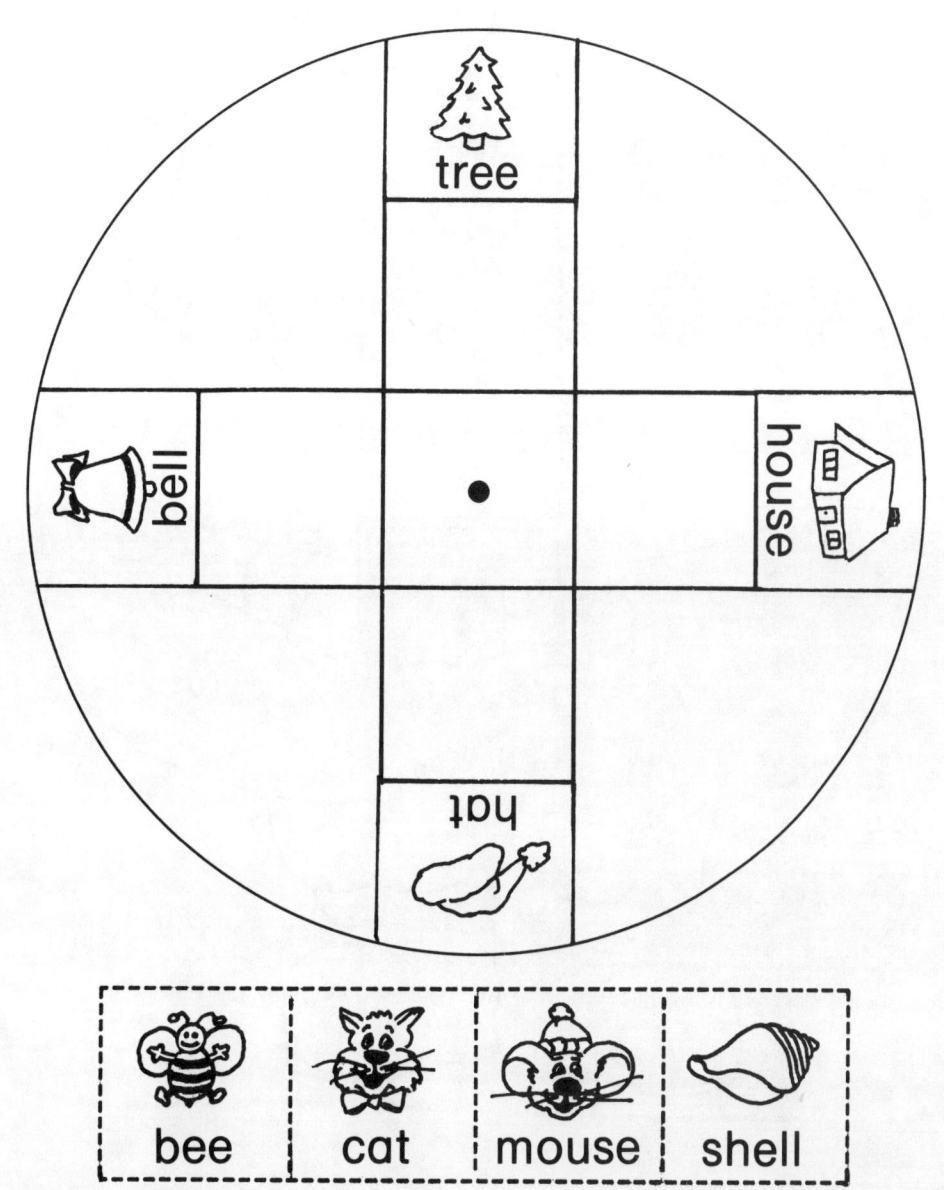

tree

bell

house

hat

bee   cat   mouse   shell

Christmas   Recognizing rhyming words • 81

Name _____

Color Santa Claus. Cut out the rectangle on the front.

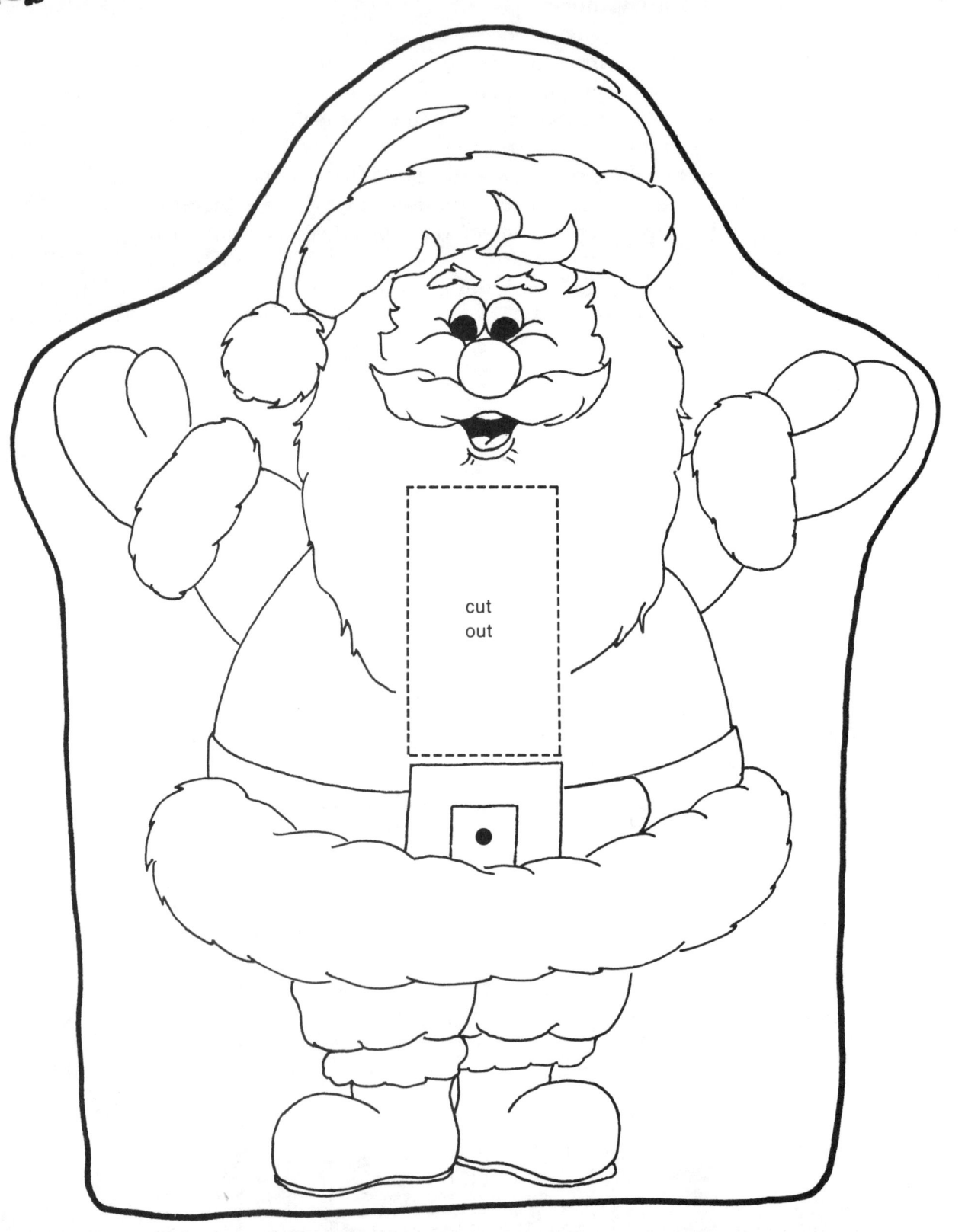

cut out

82 • Recognizing rhyming words

Christmas

Name _____

Cut out and then paste the reindeer to make pairs that look alike.

Christmas　　　　　　　　　　　　　　　　Recognizing similarities and differences • 83

Name _____

Help Santa get dressed. Cut out and then paste the numbers to show the correct order.

| 1 | 2 | 3 | 4 |

84 • Identifying sequence of events

Christmas

Name _____

Cut out and then paste the pictures to make pairs that belong together.

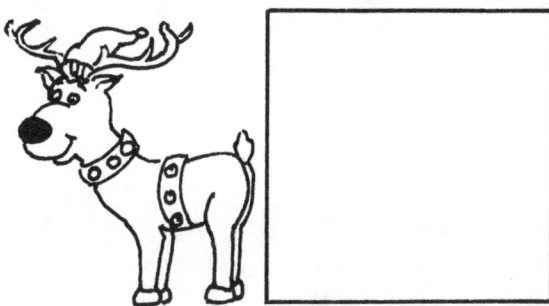

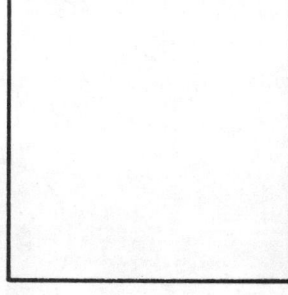

Christmas Making associations • 85

Name _____

Read the color words. Color the light bulbs.

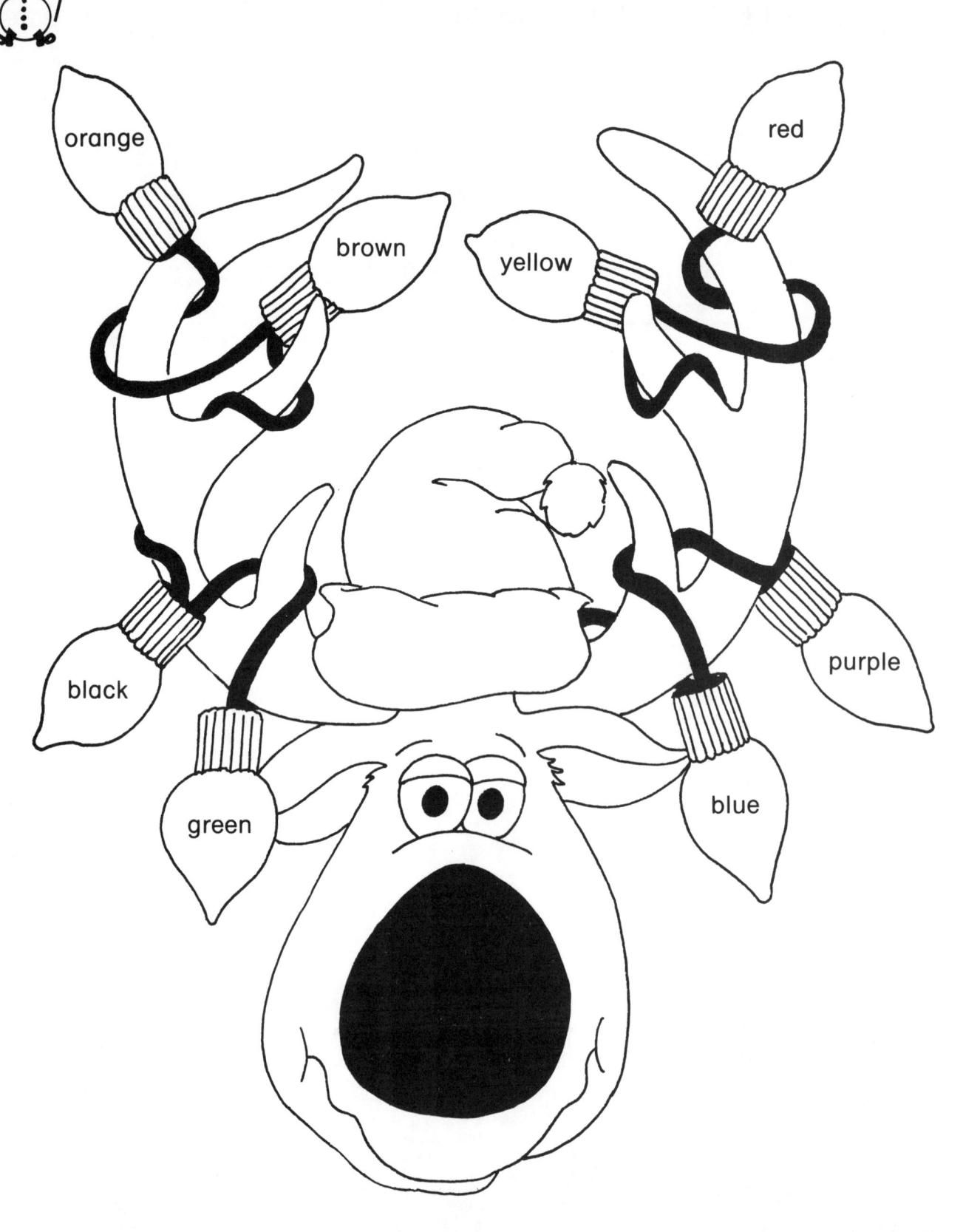

orange • brown • yellow • red • black • green • blue • purple

86 • Recognizing color words

Christmas

Name _____

Write a letter to Santa Claus.

Christmas Writing creatively • 87

Name _____

Write a story about wintertime. Use some of the words below.

boots
hats
mittens
noses
snowflakes
winter

Name _____

Cut out and then paste the pictures to match the shapes.

Christmas

Recognizing shapes • 89

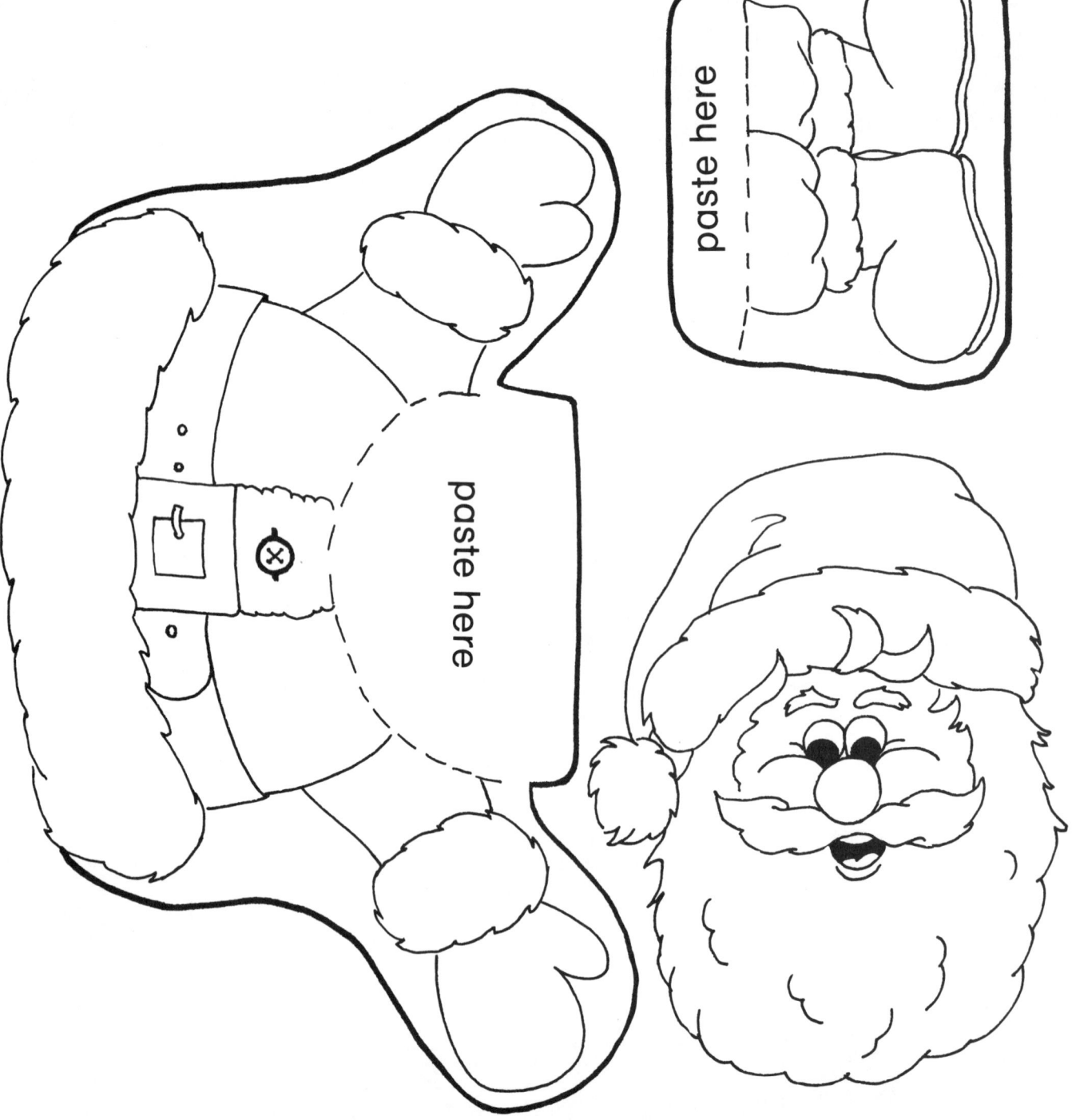

Name _____

To make the Santa Claus, do this:
Color the parts. Cut out the parts.
Paste the [face] on the [body].
Paste the [belt] on the [body].

paste here

paste here

90 • Completing an art project

Christmas

Name _____

Draw lines to connect the dots in counting order. Start with number 1. When you are finished, color the picture.

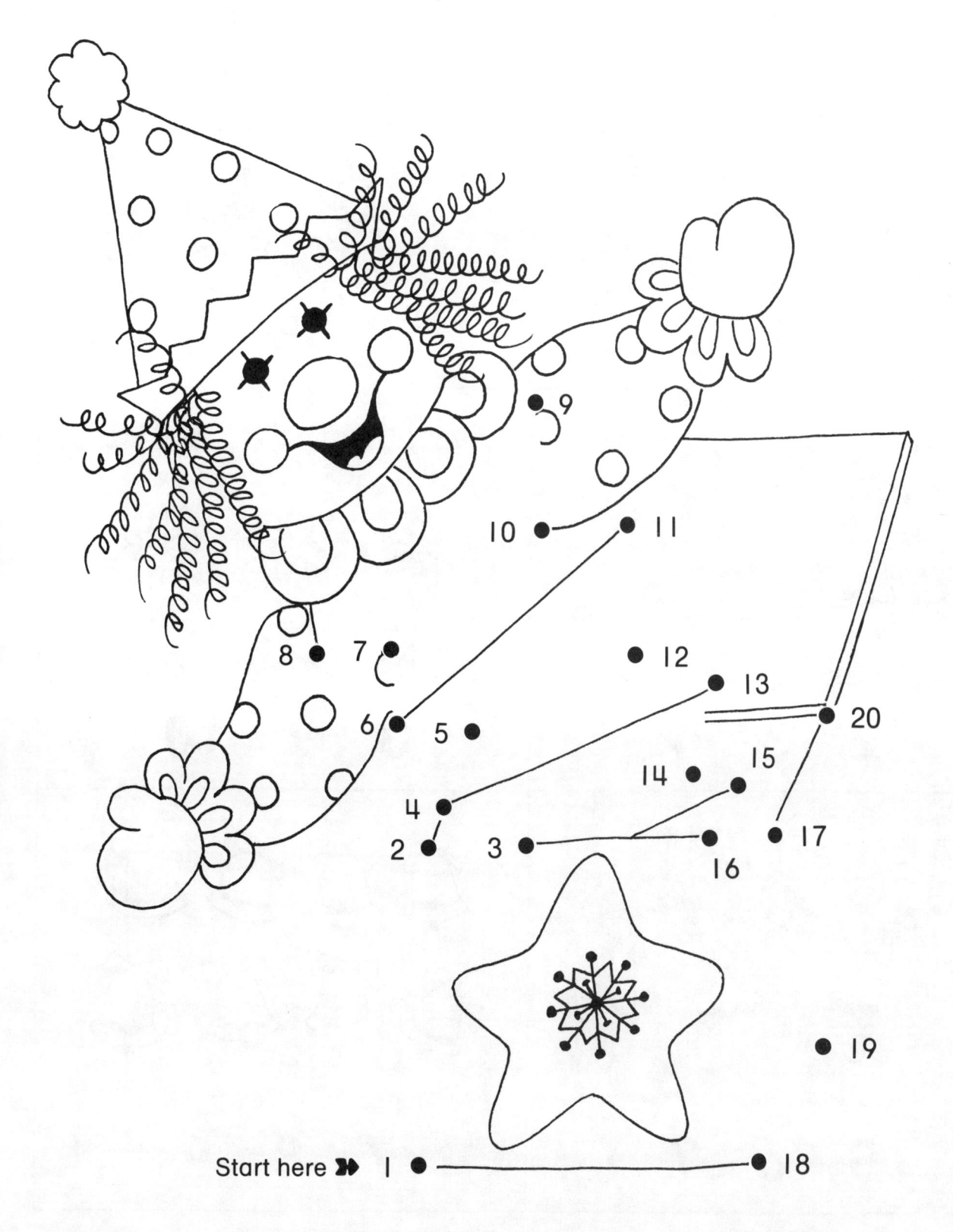

Start here ▶▶ 1

Christmas

Recognizing number sequence • 91

Name _____

Count the things in each set. Circle the number that tells how many.

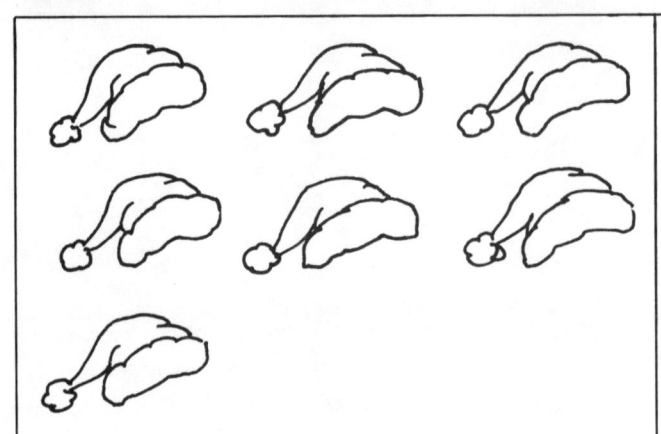

5 **6** 7	4 **5** 6
2 3 4	8 **9** 10
5 **6** 7	7 **8** 9

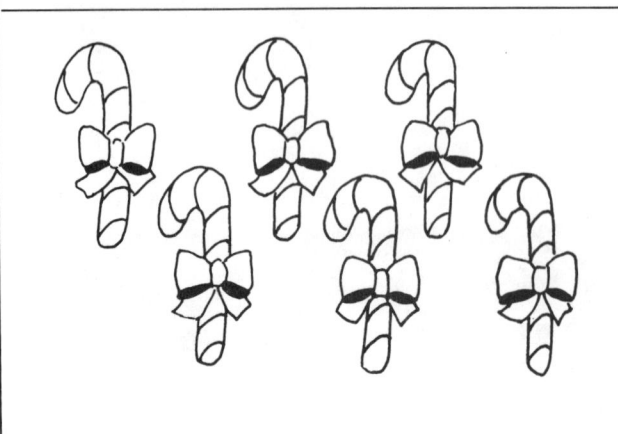

92 • Identifying number values

Christmas

Name _____

Count the things in each train car. In each answer box, write the number that tells how many.

Christmas Identifying number values • 93

Name _____

Add the numbers. As you use the answers, cross them off the stars.

2 + 6

5 + 5

2 + 2

2 + 1

3 + 2

4 + 3

7 + 2

5 + 1

1, 2, 5, 3, 4, 6, 7, 10, 8, 9

94 • Practicing addition facts less than thirteen

Christmas

Name _____

Subtract the numbers. Color each answer tree as you use it.

11 − 6 =

12 − 9 =

9 − 5 =

10 − 3 =

12 − 7 =

10 − 6 =

9 − 2 =

3

4

4

5

5

7

7

Christmas

Practicing subtraction facts less than thirteen • 95

Name _____

Sunday	Monday	Tuesday	Wednesday	Thursday	Friday	Saturday

Valentine's Day

Completing a calendar • 97

Name _____

98 • Dramatizing a poem

The Big Fearon Book of Teachers' Holiday Helpers, © 1987 David S. Lake Publishers

Valentine's Day

To the teacher:

Reproduce the activity sheet on page 100. Each student will need an activity sheet and a set of crayons in the eight basic colors. Read the directions on this sheet to your students.

Say:

Lester Lion delivers the mail to all his friends in the woods. His friends are Carmine Cat, Biffy Bear, and Daphine Duck. Listen and follow these directions as I read them aloud to you.

Start at Lester Lion.
1. Find the hearts in Lester's bag. Color them yellow.
2. Draw one blue button on Lester's jacket.
3. Lester needs a tail. Draw one long brown tail on Lester.
4. Find the path that leads to Carmine Cat. Draw four purple footprints on the path.

Look at Carmine Cat.
1. Draw a black fishing pole in Carmine's paw.
2. Draw two small orange fish in the water.
3. Color the water around the fish blue.
4. Lester gave Carmine a yellow heart. Draw it on the tree stump.
5. Find the path to Biffy Bear. Put six red footprints on the path.

Look at Biffy Bear.
1. Draw another black and yellow bee next to Biffy.
2. Biffy is standing on some blades of grass. Draw seven blades of grass under Biffy's feet.
3. Color Biffy brown.
4. Lester left a yellow heart for Biffy. Draw it on the beehive.
5. Find the path leading to Daphine Duck. Put two brown footprints on the path.

Look at Daphine Duck.
1. Put a big yellow sun in the sky above Daphine.
2. Daphine needs feet. Draw two orange circles for her feet.
3. Draw a small yellow triangle for Daphine's wing.
4. Lester left one yellow heart for Daphine. Draw it on her head.

Name _____

100 • Listening and following directions

Valentine's Day

Name _____

Cut out and then paste the pictures to make pairs of rhyming words.

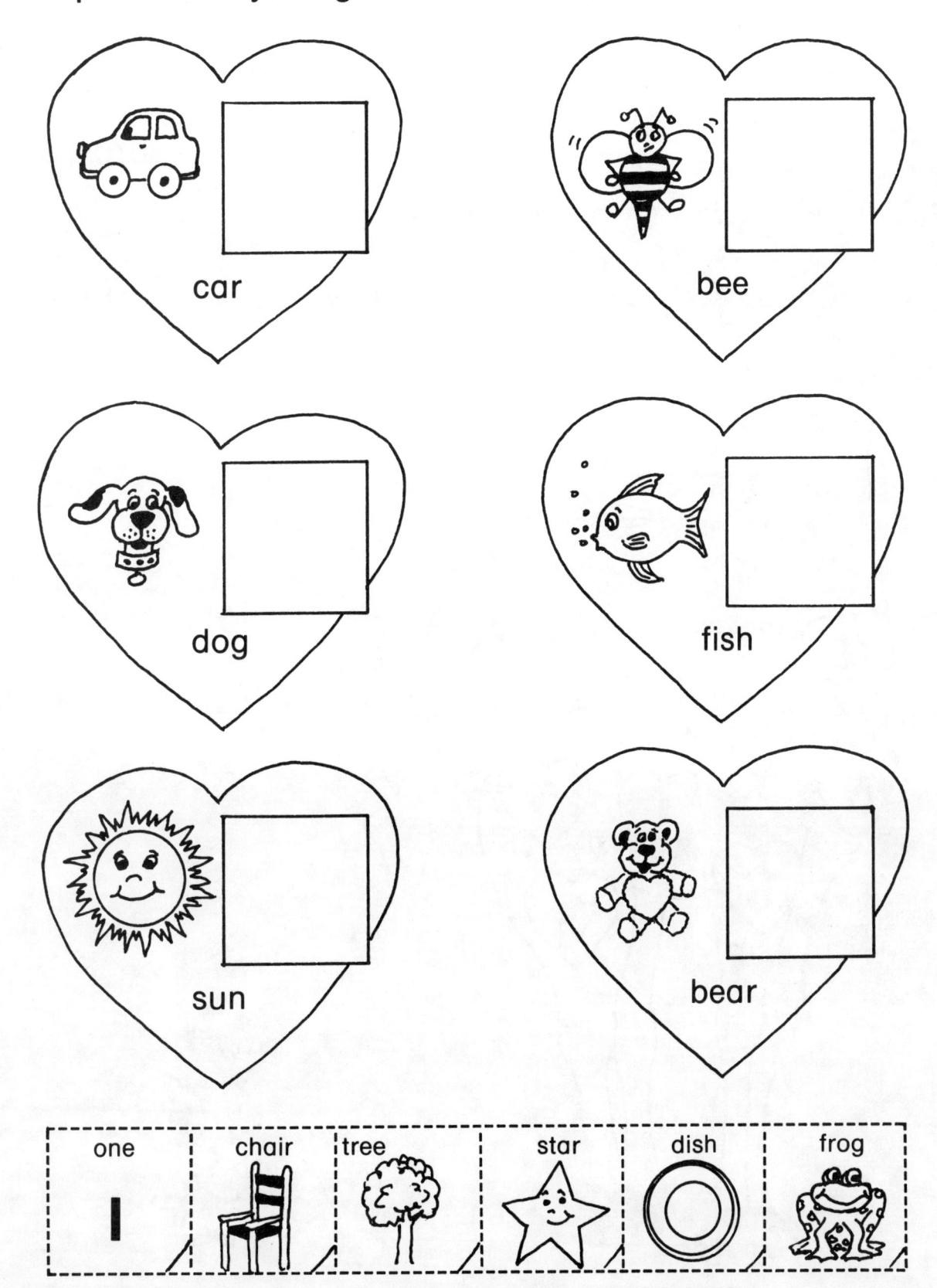

car

bee

dog

fish

sun

bear

one	chair	tree	star	dish	frog

Valentine's Day Recognizing rhyming words • 101

Name _____

Use the key. Color the hearts.

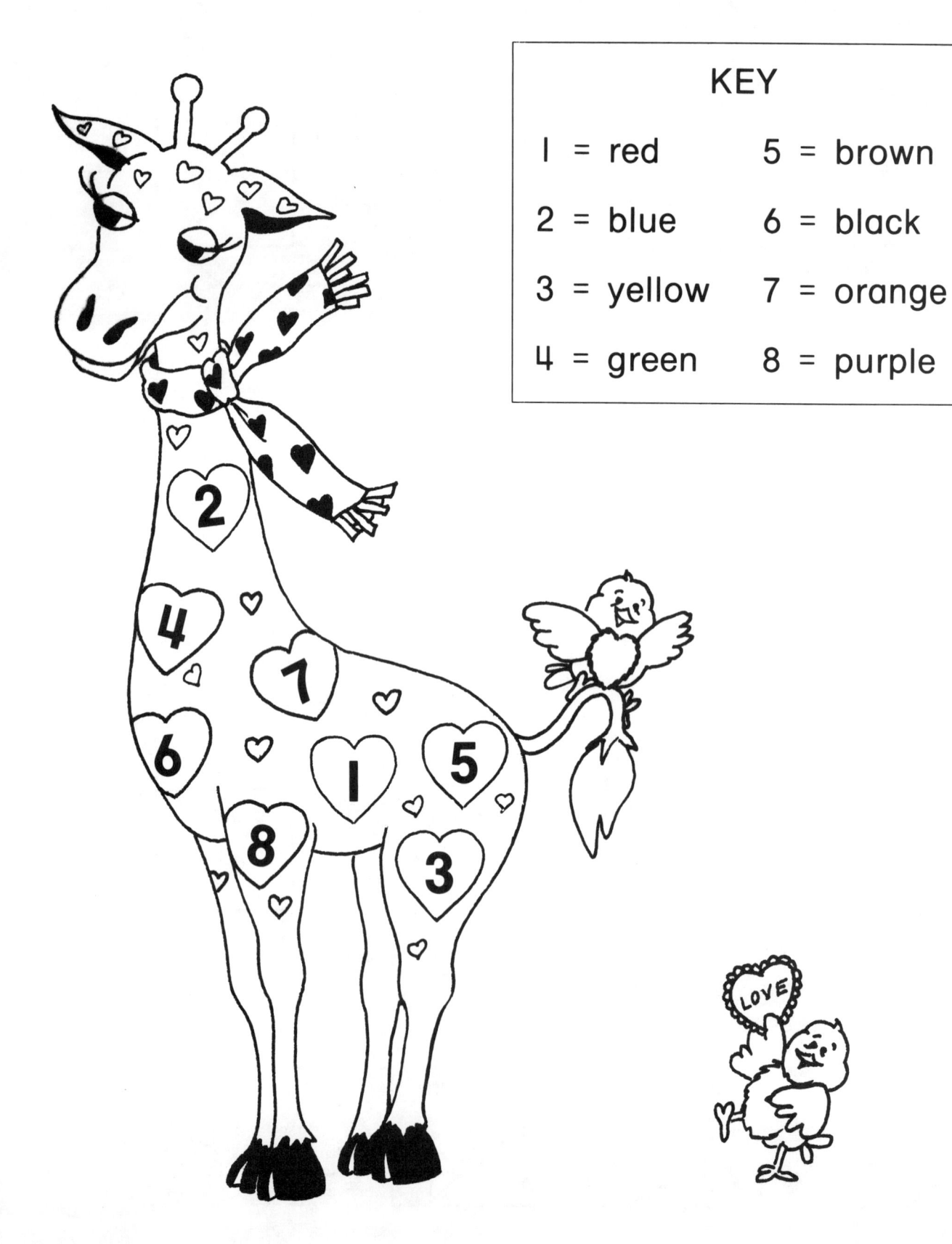

KEY

1 = red	5 = brown
2 = blue	6 = black
3 = yellow	7 = orange
4 = green	8 = purple

102 • Recognizing color words

Valentine's Day

Name _____

Find the hidden words. Circle the words in the heart as you find them.

friends

flowers

happy

heart

love

treat

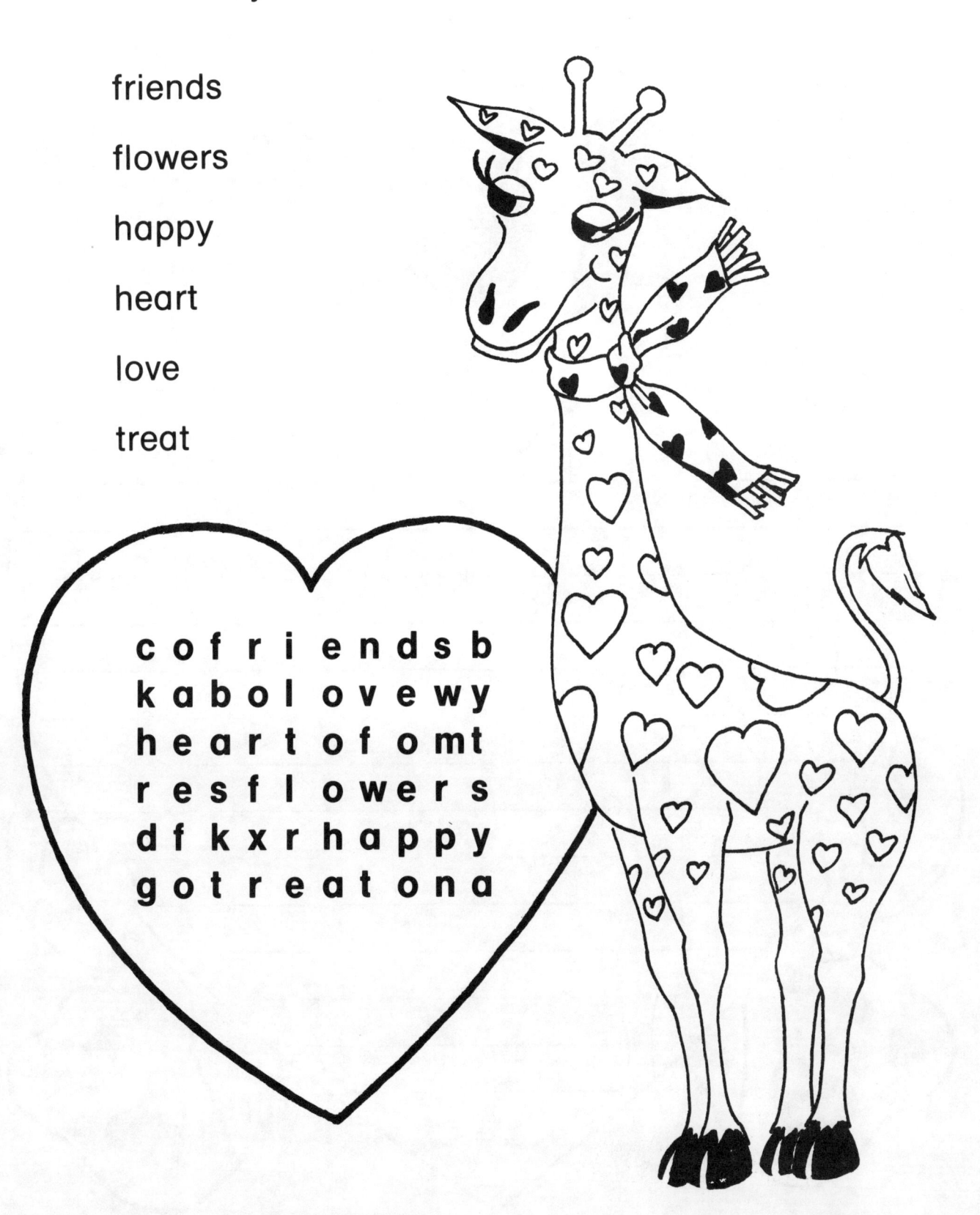

```
c o f r i e n d s b
k a b o l o v e w y
h e a r t o f o m t
r e s f l o w e r s
d f k x r h a p p y
g o t r e a t o n a
```

Valentine's Day   Finding hidden words • 103

Name _____

Write a Valentine's Day message. Use some of the words below.

be mine

happy

heart

love

please

104 • Writing creatively

Valentine's Day

Name _____

Write a story. Tell how the snail gave out her valentine cards. Use some of the words below.

glad   bunny
hurry butterfly
puppy forest
slow   friends

Valentine's Day   Writing creatively • 105

Name _____

Cut out and then paste the squares and rectangles to complete the picture.

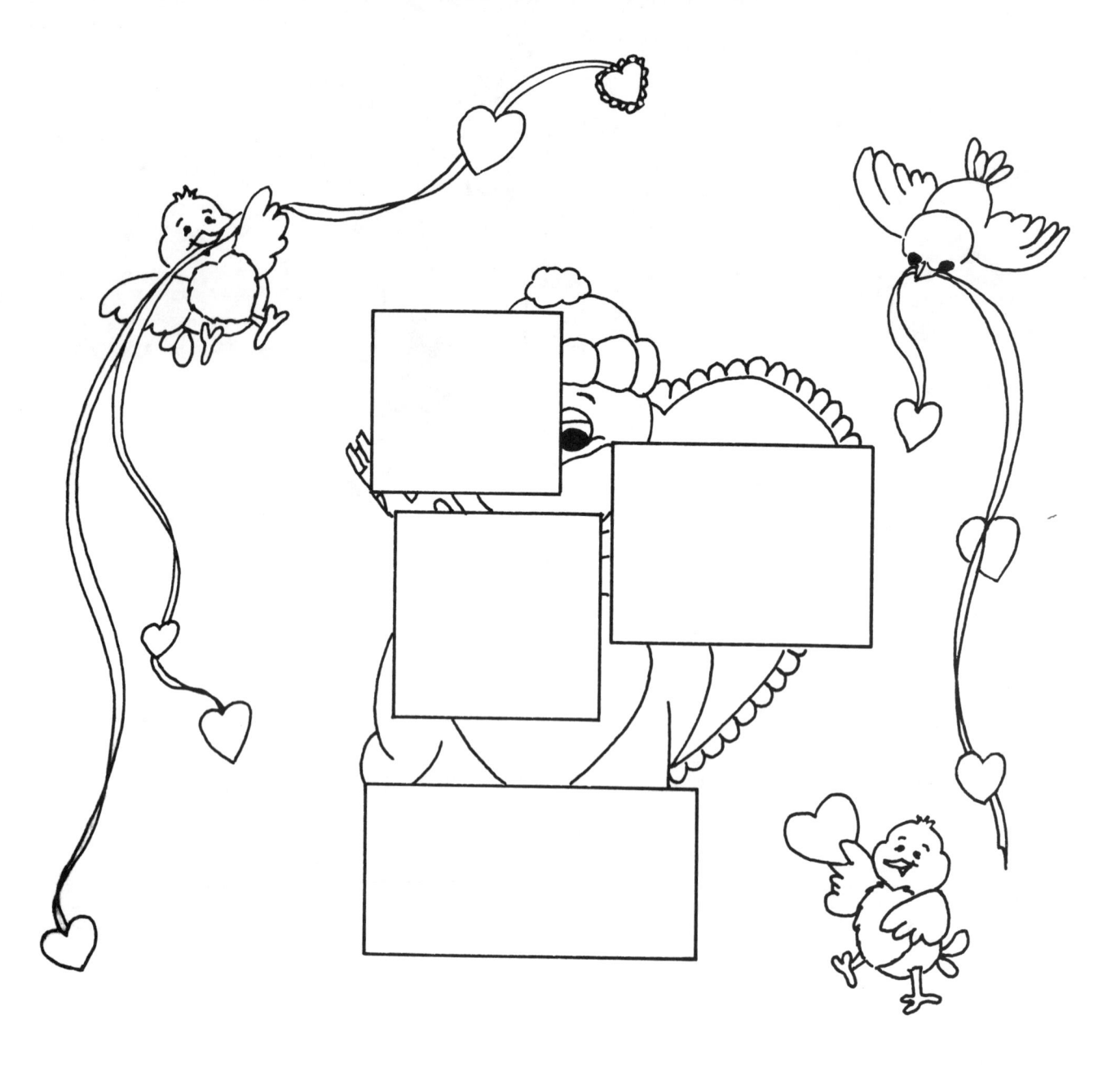

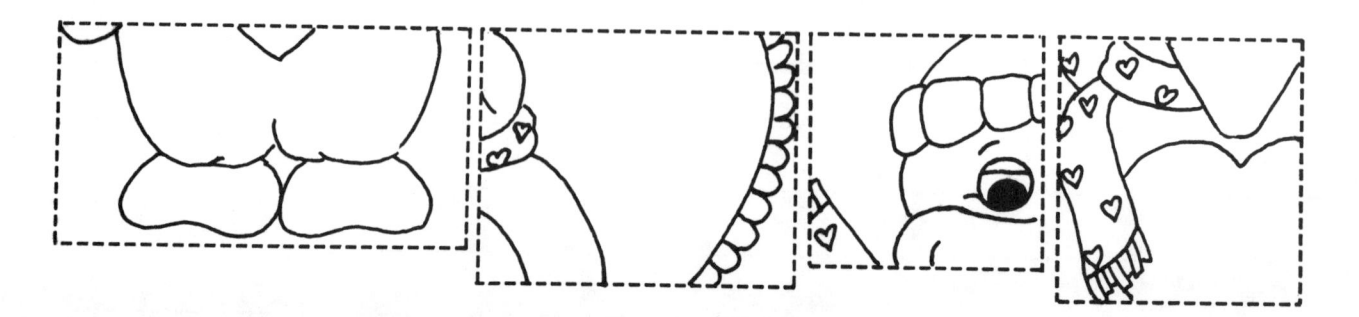

106 • Recognizing shapes

Valentine's Day

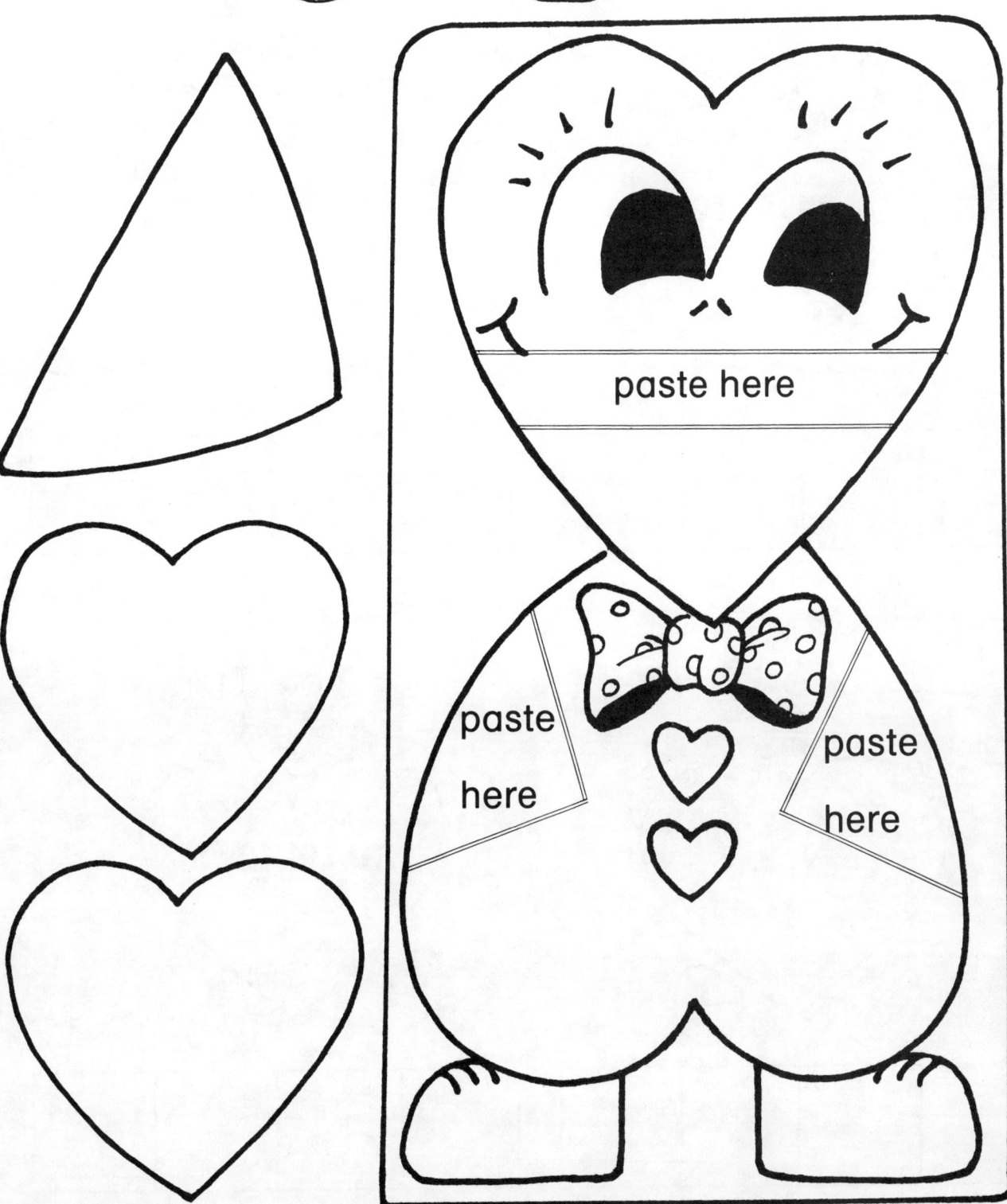

Name _____

To make the valentine bird, do this:
Color the parts. Cut out the parts.

Paste the ▽ on the 🐦 .
Paste the ♡♡ on the 🐦 .

Valentine's Day

Completing an art project • 107

Name _____

For each set of boxes, write the numbers in correct counting order.

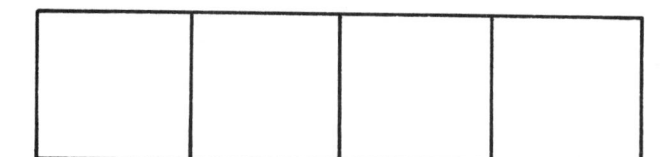

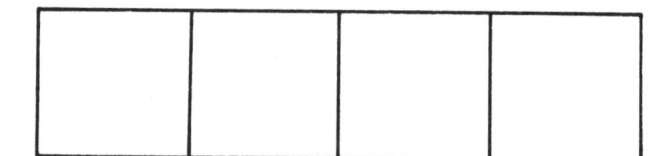

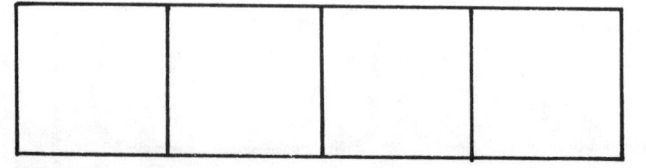

8, 11, 9, 10

12, 15, 13, 14

6, 9, 8, 7

13, 10, 12, 11

108 • Identifying number sequence

Valentine's Day

Name _____

Draw lines to connect the number words in counting order. Start with **one.** When you are finished, color the picture.

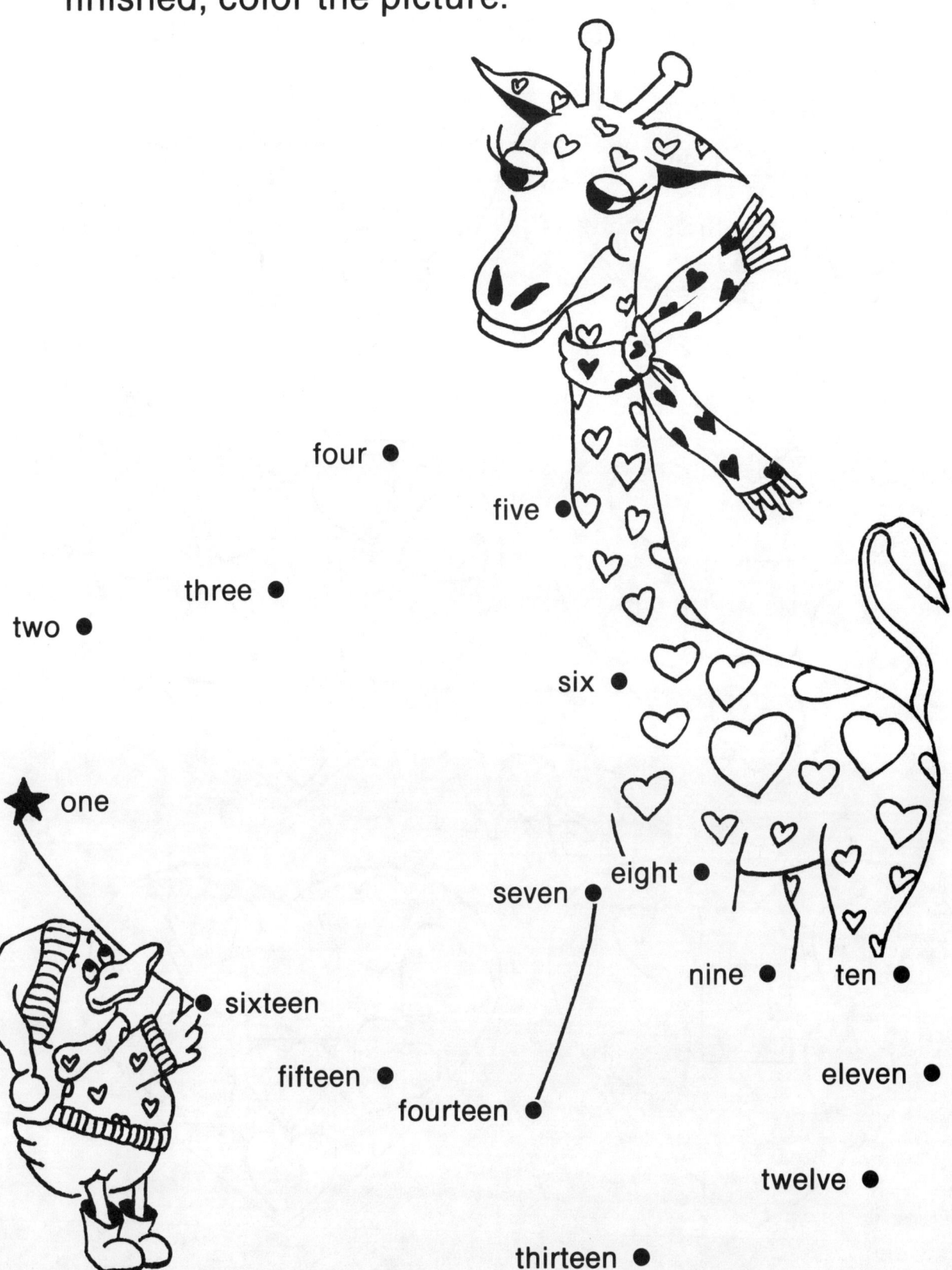

four

five

three

two

six

one

eight
seven

nine   ten

sixteen

fifteen   eleven
       fourteen

                       twelve

     thirteen

Valentine's Day Recognizing number words and number sequence • 109

Name _____

For each big heart, count the little hearts. In the boxes, write the numbers that tell how many.

110 • Identifying number values

Valentine's Day

Name _____

Add the numbers. Color each answer apple as you use it.

4	2	8	6	7
+ 5	+ 8	+ 5	+ 5	+ 7
□	□	□	□	□

6	5	8	9	6
+ 2	+ 7	+ 9	+ 7	+ 9
□	□	□	□	□

8   9   10   11   12

13   14   15   16   17

Valentine's Day   Practicing addition facts less than eighteen • 111

Name _____

Add the numbers. Color each answer heart as you use it.

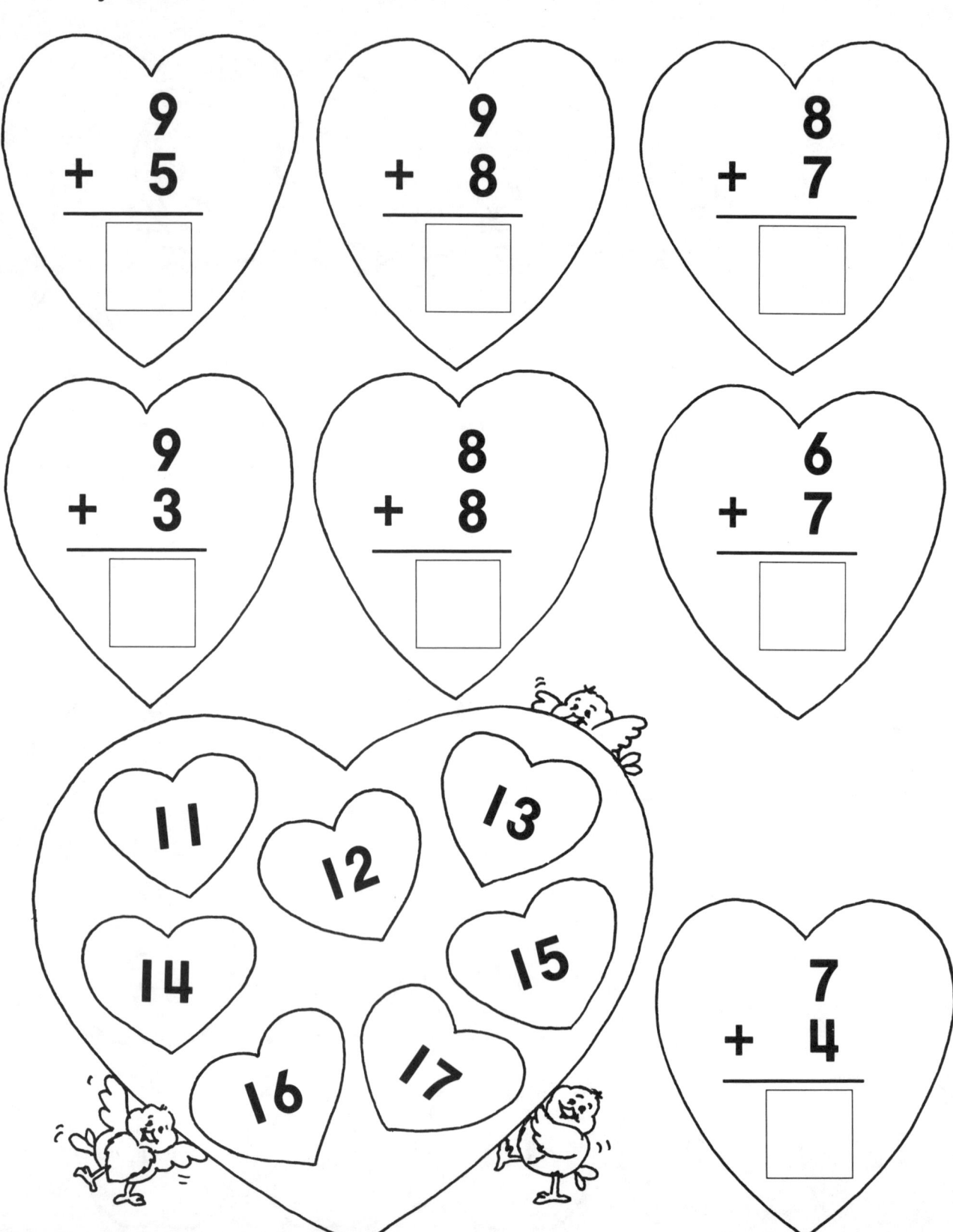

9 + 5

9 + 8

8 + 7

9 + 3

8 + 8

6 + 7

11 12 13
14 15
16 17

7 + 4

112 • Practicing addition facts less than eighteen

Valentine's Day

Name _____

Subtract the numbers and write the answers.
Use the key and color the bones.

KEY

2 = yellow
3 = purple
4 = orange
5 = green
6 = blue
7 = brown
8 = red

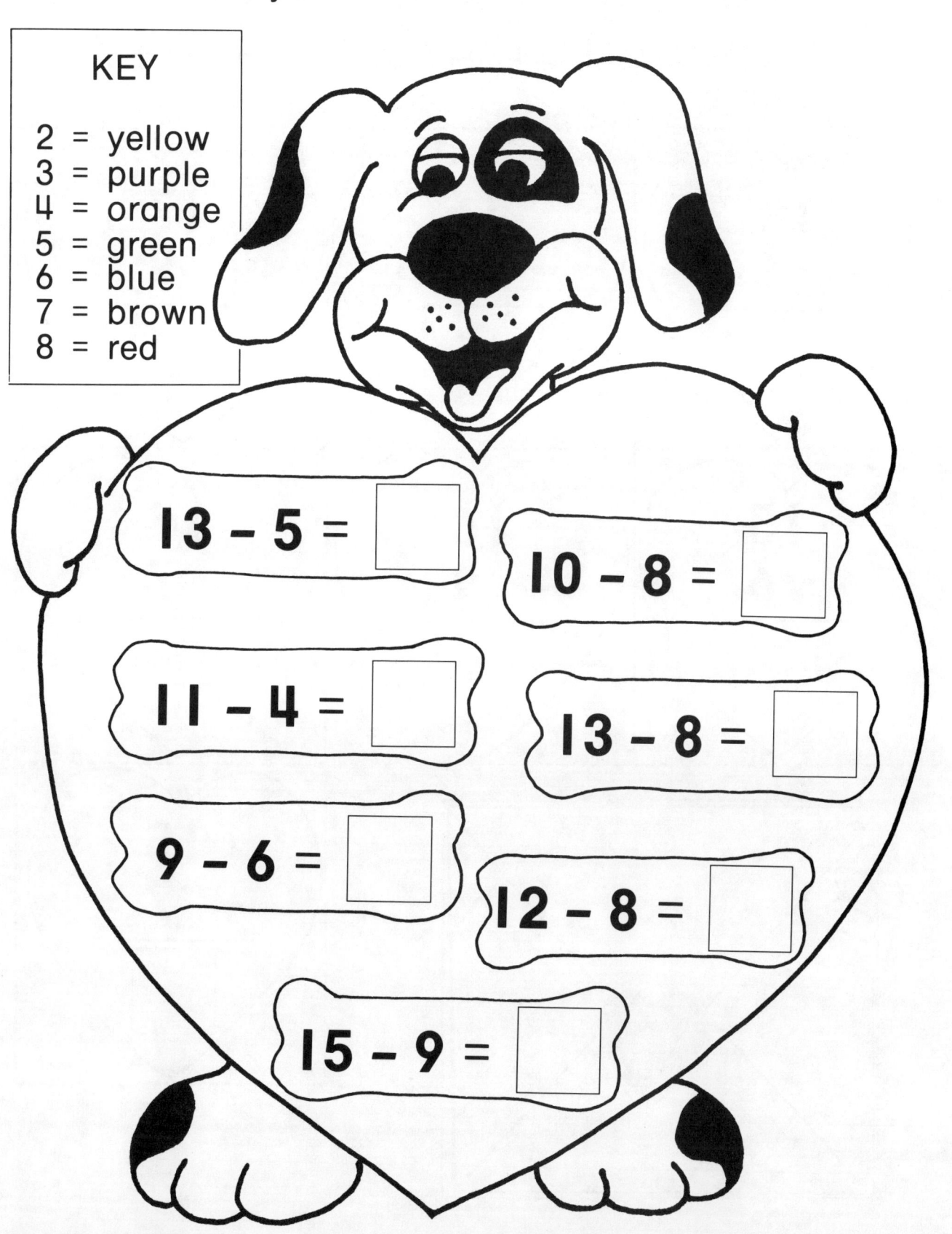

13 – 5 =

10 – 8 =

11 – 4 =

13 – 8 =

9 – 6 =

12 – 8 =

15 – 9 =

Valentine's Day   Practicing subtraction facts less than eighteen • 113

Name. _____

Subtract the numbers. Write the answers.

Color the ✉ .

Cut on all the dotted lines. Use the parts on the next page.

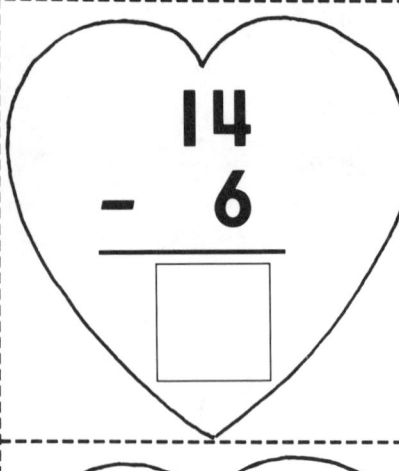

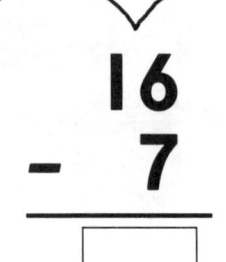

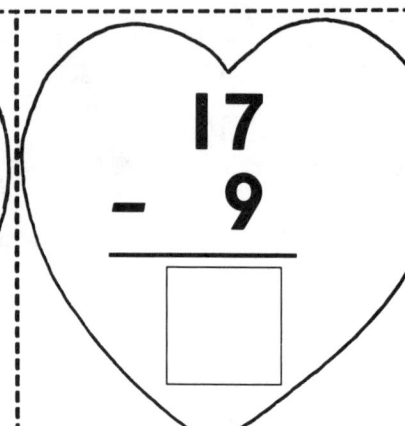

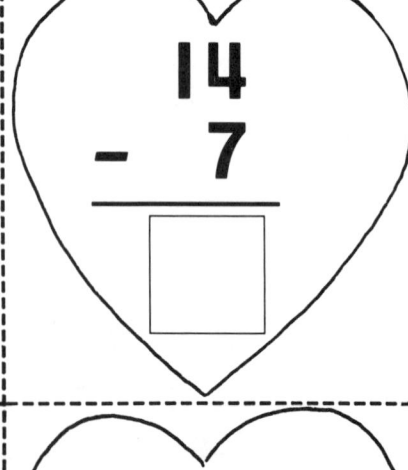

14 − 6 =

16 − 7 =

17 − 9 =

15 − 6 =

16 − 9 =

14 − 7 =

15 − 7 =

114 • Practicing subtraction facts less than eighteen

Valentine's Day

Name _____

Use the parts from the subtraction page. Do this:
Color the picture.

Paste the ✉ on the 🐢.

Put the hearts in the pocket.

paste here

paste here

paste here

Valentine's Day

Completing a math project • 115

Name _____

Solve the problems. Cut out and then paste the correct answers to complete each heart.

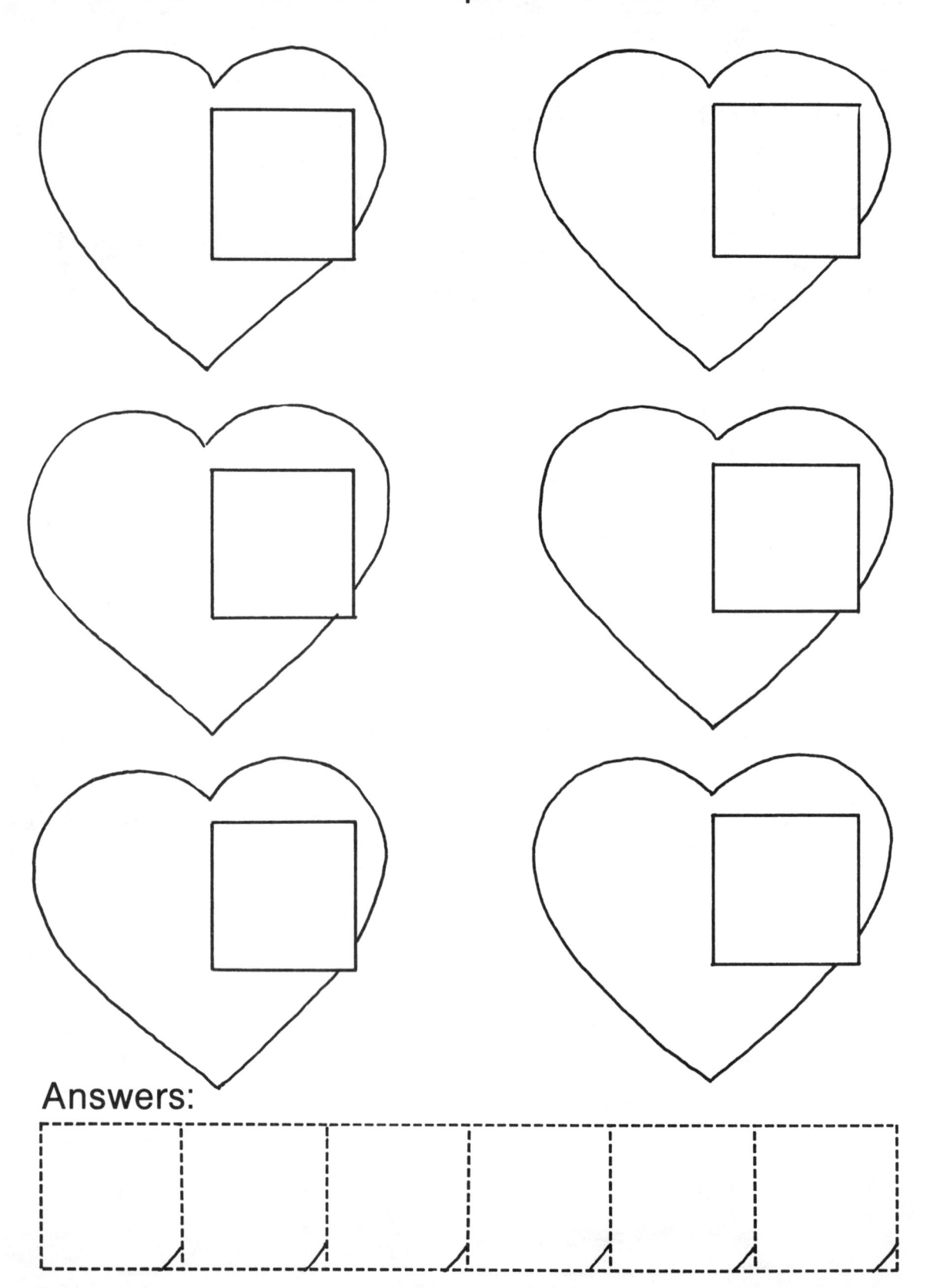

Answers:

116 • Solving equations

Valentine's Day

Name _____

Solve the problems. As you use each answer, cross it off the big answer heart below.

Answers:

Valentine's Day Solving equations • 117

Name _____

Sunday	Monday	Tuesday	Wednesday	Thursday	Friday	Saturday

Springtime

Completing a calendar • 119

Name _____

paste here

120 • Dramatizing a poem

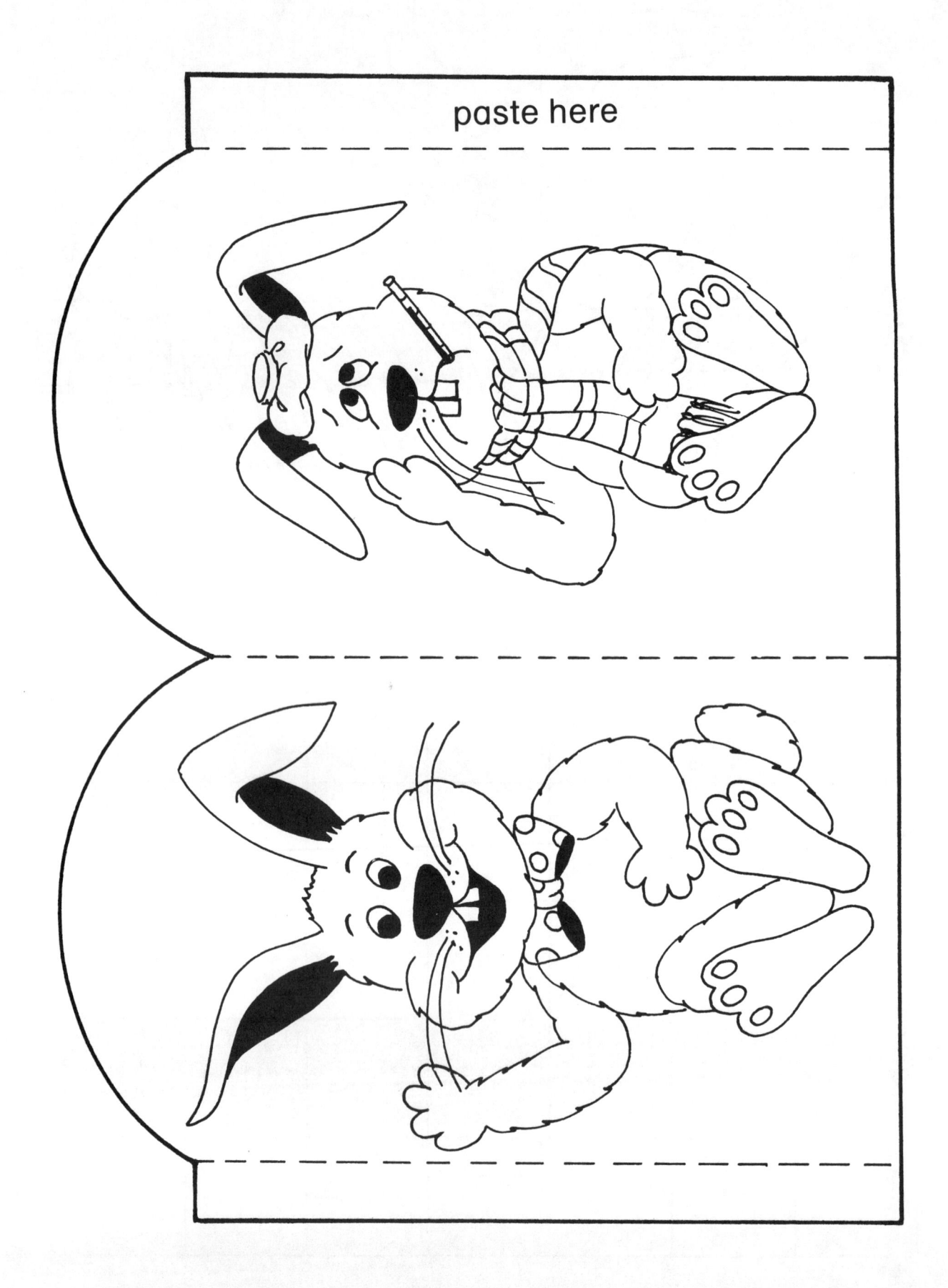

Springtime

To the teacher:

Reproduce the activity sheet on page 122. Each student will need an activity sheet and a set of crayons in the eight basic colors. Read the directions on this sheet to your students.

Say:

Listen and follow the directions as I read them aloud to you.

Row 1
1. Find the bunny that is hiding beside the chicken. Color the bunny brown.
2. Put a big blue X on the chicken that is looking down.
3. Find the pile of eggs. Count the eggs and write the number in the box. Color each egg a different color.

Row 2
1. Find the bunny that is sitting down. Color her yellow.
2. Draw a green triangle around the duck.
3. Count all the eggs in the row. On the pail of paint, write the number of eggs.

Row 3
1. Count the eggs in the bunny's cart. Write the number on the wheel.
2. Color one bunny blue and one bunny yellow.
3. Put a green rectangle around the pile of six eggs. Color the eggs.

• 121

Name _____

1

2

3

122 • Listening and following directions

Springtime

Name _____

Say the name of each picture. Cut out and then paste the beginning sound letters.

ar

ider

y

ee

ail

ate

| fl | sk | sn | sp | st | tr |

Springtime Identifying initial blends • 123

Name _____

Find the hidden words. Circle the words in the ice cream as you find them.

```
d f r s m i l e y n
o c l o u d e q u p
r s i b c l k s u n
r a i n t y u i o p
y a d o w i n d l l
e s p r i n g t u v
```

cloud

rain

smile

spring

sun

wind

124 • Finding hidden words

Springtime

Name _____

❁ Read the sentence on the line below. Then read the sentences in the box. To finish the story, write the sentences in order.

> First he will eat.
>
> Now Biffy is up.
>
> Then he will play.

Biffy was sleeping.

Springtime

Recognizing story sequence • 125

Name _____

✿ Write a story. Tell what you like to do on a rainy day. Use some of the words below.

fun

indoors

play

puddles

raincoat

umbrella

Name _____

Write a story about springtime.

Springtime

Name _____

Write a greeting on the egg. Color the egg. Cut out the egg. Fold it on the dotted lines. Draw and color a picture on the outside of the egg. Use the bunny parts on the next page to finish the greeting card.

128 • Completing an art project

Springtime

Name _____

To make the bunny card, use the bunny parts and the egg greeting that you have made. Do this:

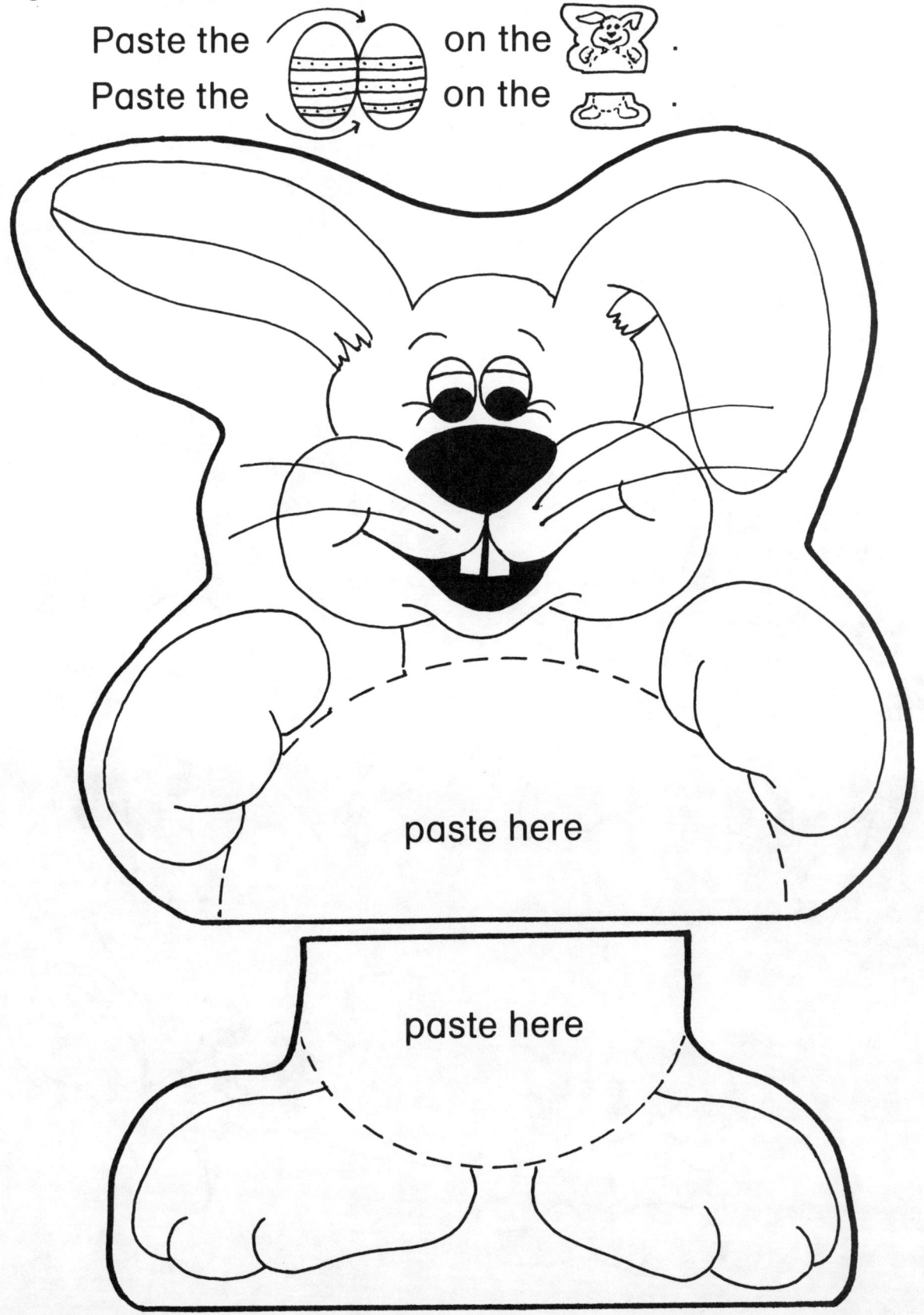

Paste the 🥚🥚 on the 🐰.
Paste the 🥚🥚 on the 👣.

paste here

paste here

Springtime

Completing an art project • 129

Name _____

Draw lines to connect the dots in counting order. Start with number **1**. When you are finished, color the picture.

130 • Recognizing number sequence

Springtime

Name _____

In the boxes on each cloud, write the numbers in counting order.

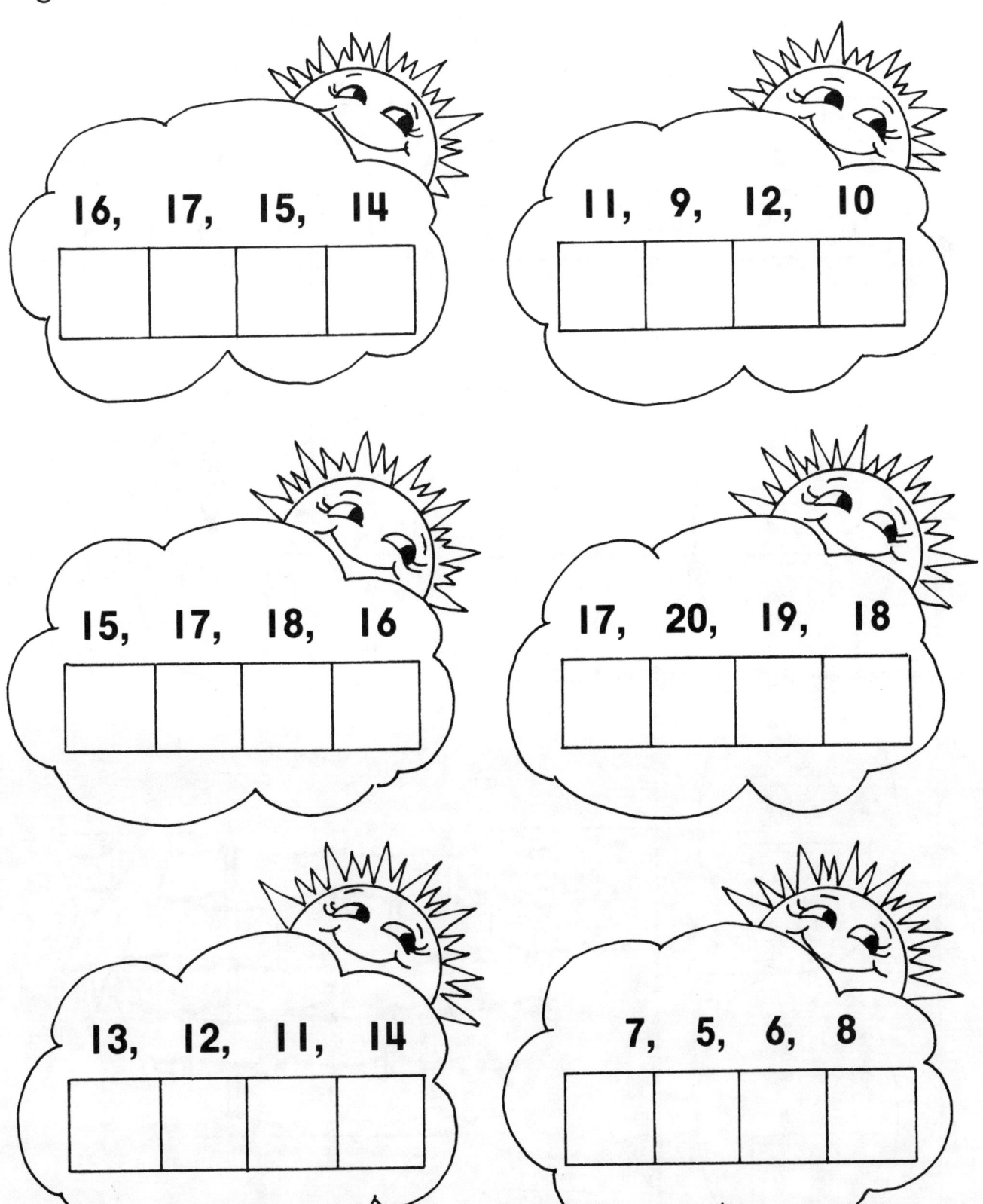

16, 17, 15, 14

11, 9, 12, 10

15, 17, 18, 16

17, 20, 19, 18

13, 12, 11, 14

7, 5, 6, 8

Springtime

Identifying number sequence • 131

Name _____

❋ Add the numbers. Write the answers.
Color the 🧺. 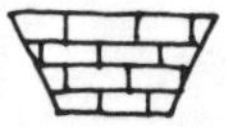
Cut on all the dotted lines. Use the bunny on the next page to make a springtime basket.

6 + 8 =

5 + 8 =

9 + 6 =

7 + 9 =

6 + 6 =

2 + 9 =

5 + 5 =

2 + 7 =

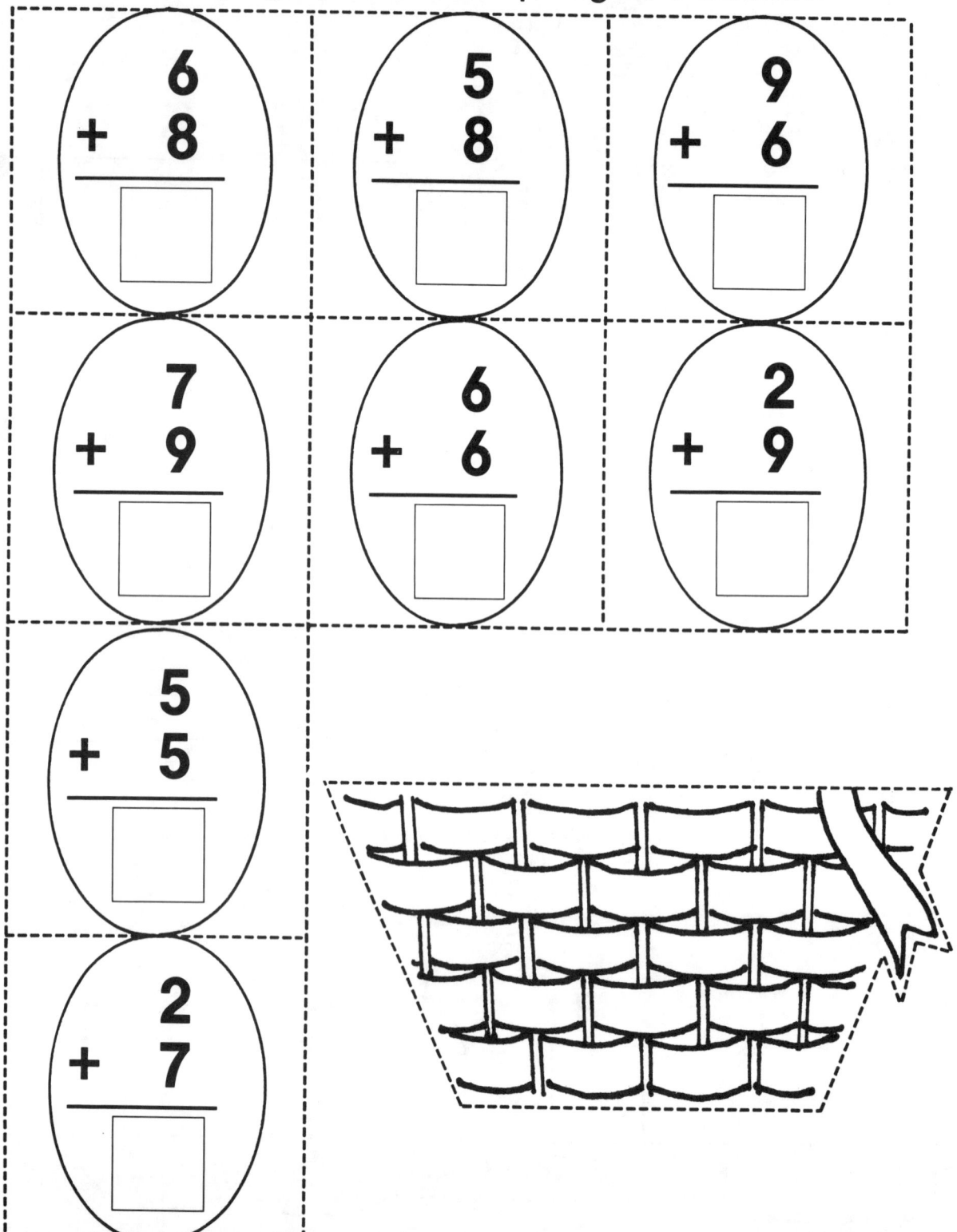

132 • Practicing addition facts less than eighteen

Springtime

Name _____

Use the parts from the addition page. Do this:
Color the picture.

Paste the 🧺 on the 🐰. Put the eggs in the pocket.

paste here   paste here
paste here

Springtime   Completing a math project • 133

Name _____

❋ Add the numbers. Cut out and then paste the numbers to complete each umbrella.

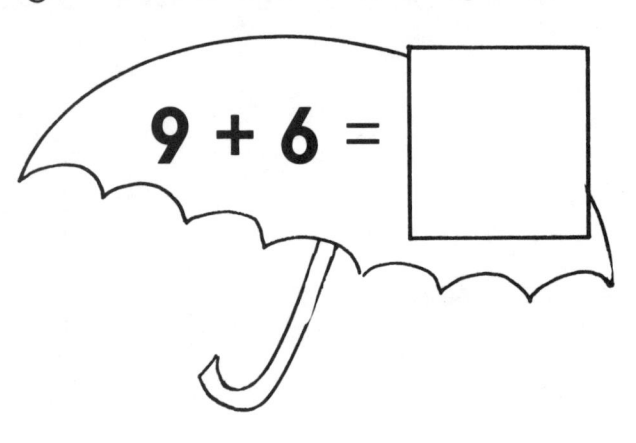

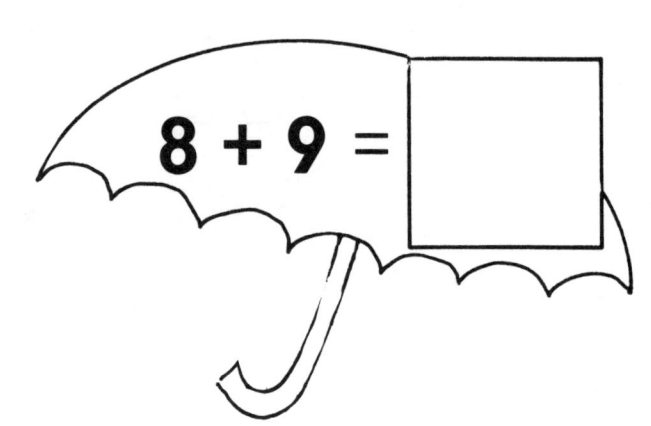

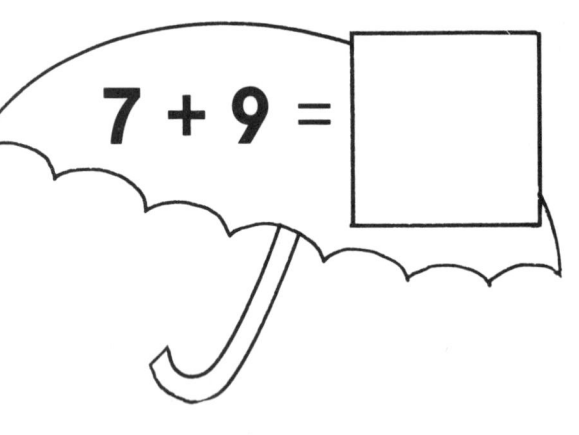

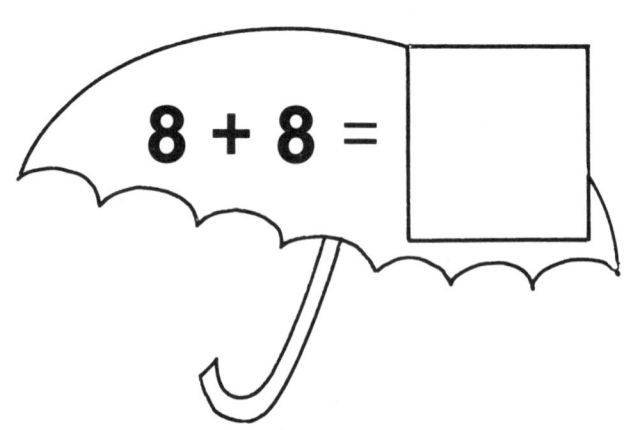

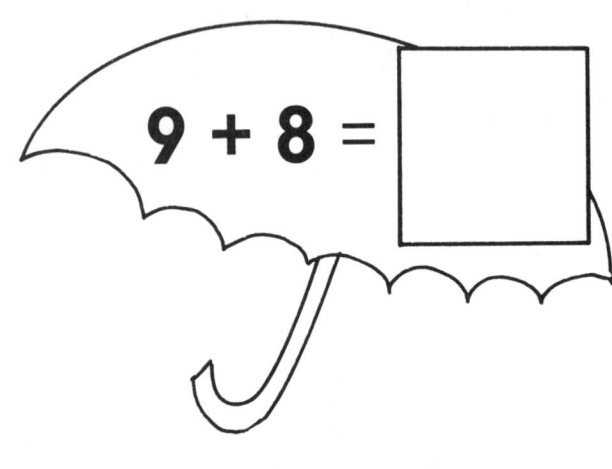

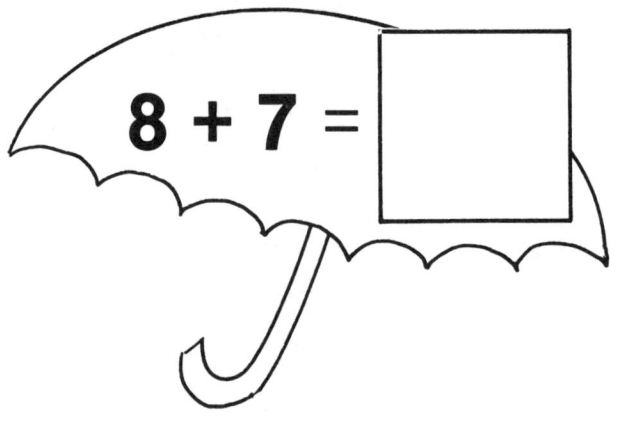

9 + 6 =

8 + 9 =

7 + 9 =

8 + 8 =

9 + 8 =

8 + 7 =

| 15 | 15 | 16 | 16 | 17 | 17 |

Practicing addition facts less than eighteen

Springtime

Name _____

Use the problems in the cloud to complete the number sentences in the raindrops.

12 − 7   11 − 5
10 − 4   12 − 5
11 − 3   10 − 2
13 − 8   14 − 7

☐ − ☐ = 8
☐ − ☐ = 8

☐ − ☐ = 7
☐ − ☐ = 7

☐ − ☐ = 6
☐ − ☐ = 6

☐ − ☐ = 5
☐ − ☐ = 5

Springtime   Practicing subtraction facts less than eighteen • 135

Name _____

Subtract the numbers. Color each answer tulip as you use it.

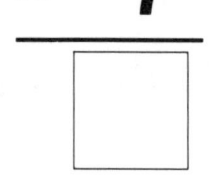

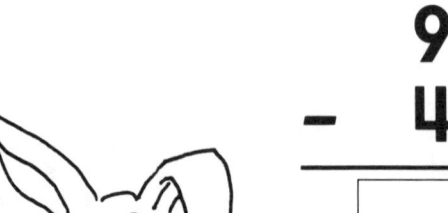

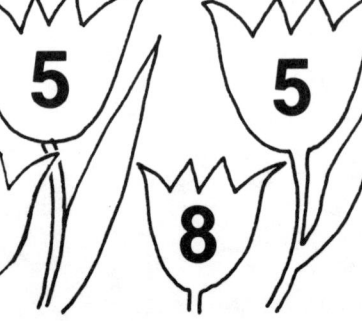

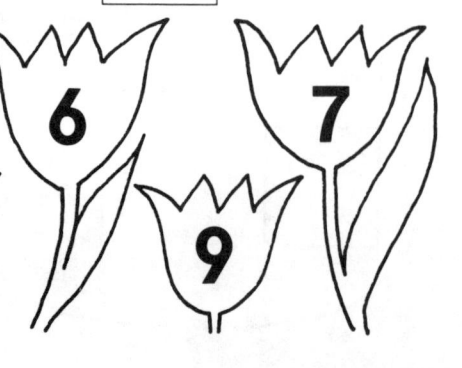

16 − 7 = ☐

12 − 6 = ☐

12 − 5 = ☐

14 − 6 = ☐

16 − 8 = ☐

9 − 4 = ☐

11 − 2 = ☐

15 − 8 = ☐

11 − 5 = ☐

13 − 8 = ☐

5 5 6 6 7
7 8 8 9 9

136 • Practicing subtraction facts less than eighteen

Springtime

Name _____

✿ Solve the problems. As you use each answer, cross it off the big bone below.

Answers

Springtime   Solving equations • 137

Name _____

Solve the problems. As you use each answer, cross it off the rain cloud below.

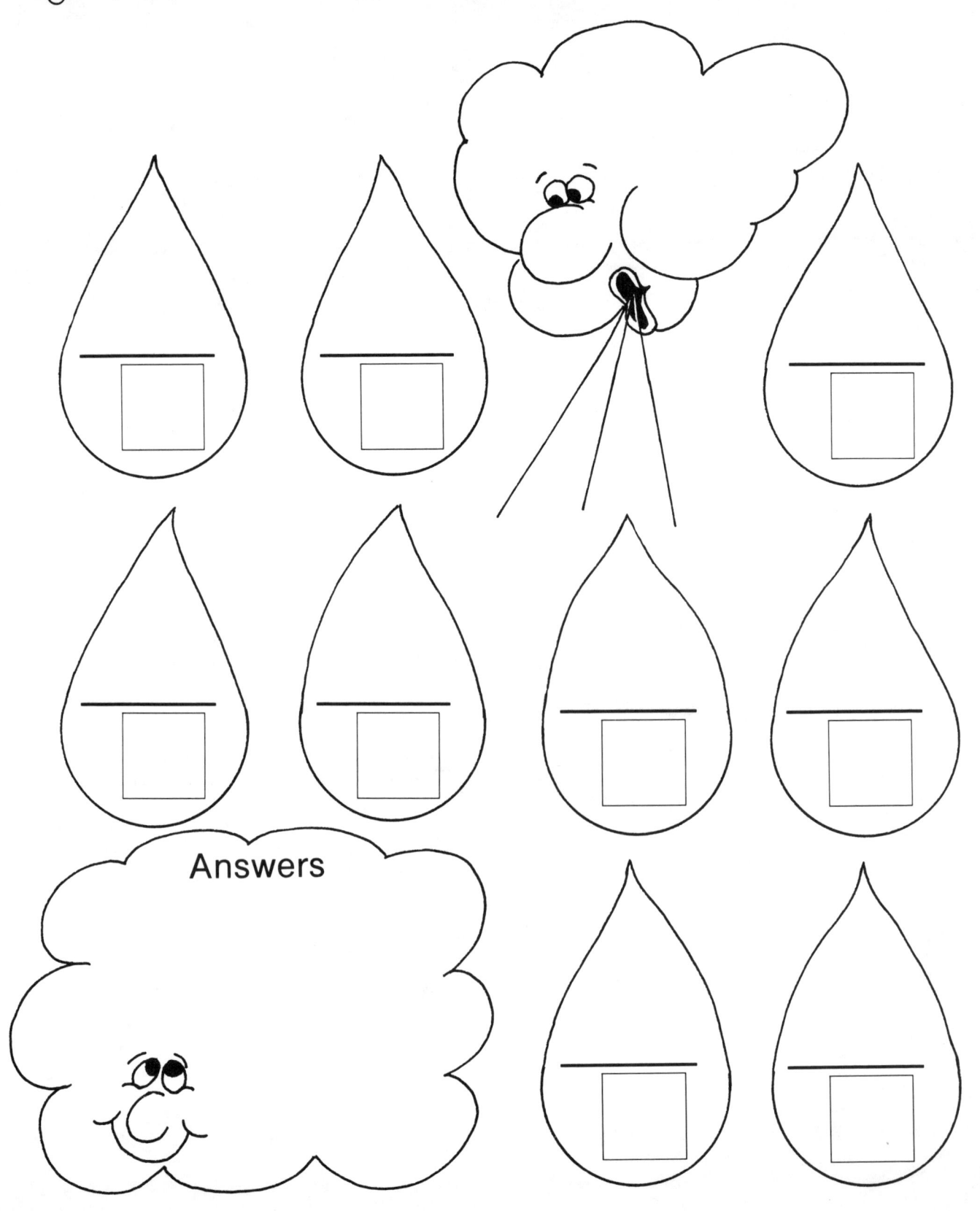

Answers

138 • Solving equations

Springtime

Name _____

Solve the problems. As you use each answer, cross it off the big ladybug below.

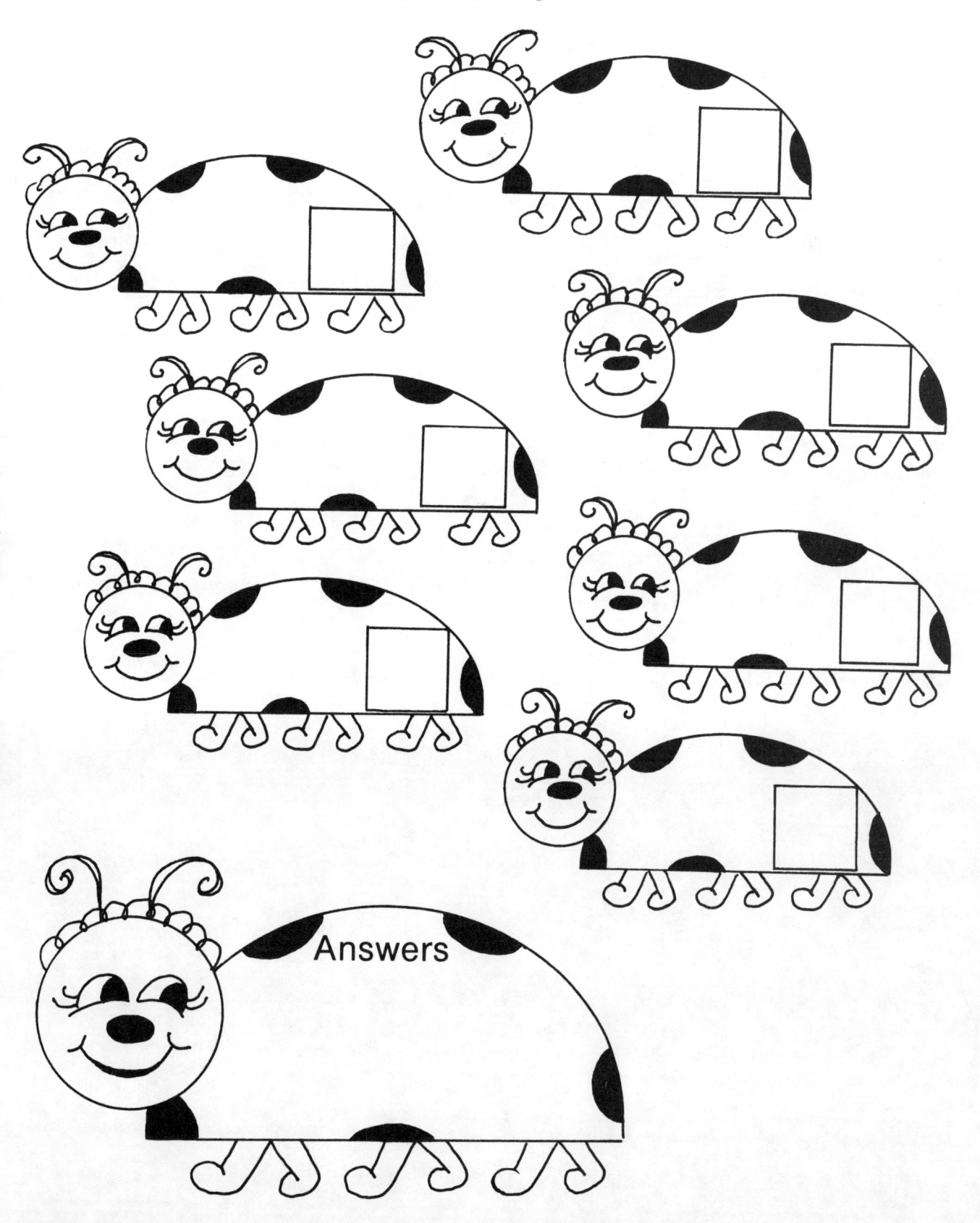

Springtime

Solving equations • 139